Best
Practices *for*
High School
Classrooms

Randi Stone

Best
Practices *for*
High School
Classrooms

What
Award-Winning
Secondary
Teachers Do

CORWIN PRESS, INC.
A Sage Publications Company
Thousand Oaks, California

For information:

Corwin Press, Inc.
A Sage Publications Company
2455 Teller Road
Thousand Oaks, California 91320
E-mail: order@corwinpress.com

Sage Publications Ltd.
6 Bonhill Street
London EC2A 4PU
United Kingdom

Sage Publications India Pvt. Ltd.
M-32 Market
Greater Kailash I
New Delhi 110 048 India

Printed in the United States of America

Library of Congress Cataloging-in-Publication Data

Stone, Randi.
    Best practices for high school classrooms: What award-winning secondary teachers do / by Randi Stone.
        p. cm.
    Includes bibliographical references and index.
    ISBN 0-7619-7729-5 (c) — ISBN 0-7619-7730-9 (p)
    1. High school teachers—United States—Case studies. 2. High school teaching—United States—Case studies.   I. Title.
    LB1777.2 .S76 2001
    373.1102—dc21   2001002166

02   03   04   05   06   07   7   6   5   4   3   2   1

Acquiring Editor:	Faye Zucker
Corwin Editorial Assistant:	Julia Parnell
Production Editor:	Diane S. Foster
Editorial Assistant:	Cindy Bear
Copy Editor:	Rachel Hile Bassett
Typesetter/Designer:	Denyse Dunn
Proofer:	Joyce Kuhn
Indexer:	Sheila Bodell
Cover Designer:	Michelle Lee

Contents

Preface

The attention for my last book, *Best Classroom Practices: What Award-Winning Elementary Teachers Do* (Corwin Press, 1999), motivated me to provide the same resource for high school teachers. Thus *Best Practices for High School Classrooms: What Award-Winning Secondary Teachers Do* was born. Designed to be a helpful book for practicing as well as future teachers, this unique guide provides exemplary teaching practices from outstanding educators who are willing to share their expertise. It is an instant network of people, projects, ideas, and helpful tips. Once again, I used a "poke my nose into classrooms" technique to talk with award-winning teachers and to listen to them talk about what they are doing in their own classrooms. These are the teachers we read about in journals and magazines, the teachers who win grants, fellowships, and contests. I hope you enjoy "poking your nose" into their classrooms as much as I did. Teachers from all over the country sent me their exemplary projects, ideas, and helpful tips. Opening my mail was such a joy! Now, it's your turn to enjoy all of the wonderful information that I have been privileged to read.

▨ Who Should Read This Book

This book is for practicing and future high school educators. Although it is designed for teachers, this could also be a resource for administrators interested in discovering what outstanding educators are doing across the country.

⧉ Where to Begin

The chapters are divided by subject area. Go right to your area, or skip around. You are certain to learn so much from your colleagues!

⧉ Acknowledgments

I thank all the award-winning teachers across the country who submitted their work for this publication. Grateful acknowledgment is also made to the contributors for special permission to use their material. All rights are reserved.

About the Author

Randi Stone is a graduate of Clark University, Boston University, and Salem State College. She holds credentials for elementary education, and she recently completed her Ed.D. at the University of Massachusetts, Lowell. Stone is author of a previous book with Corwin Press, *Best Classroom Practices: What Award-Winning Elementary Teachers Do* (1999).

About the Contributors

Douglas L. Bailer, Teacher
Pisgah High School
60 Metcalf Street
Pisgah, AL 35765
School telephone: (256) 451-3241
e-mail: bailerdl@JacksonK12.org

Awards: Appointed by Governor Don Siegleman of Alabama to the
Teacher Preparedness Advisory Panel, 2000
Received National Board for Professional Teaching Stan-
dards Certification in Adolescent and Young Adulthood
Mathematics, 1999

Jean E. (Keppel) Baldikoski, English Teacher
Naperville Central High School
440 W. Aurora Avenue
Naperville, IL 60540-6298

Awards: Fellow in Writing, University of Chicago, 1997
Kohl Academy International Teaching Award, 1995
Fulbright Exchange Teacher to Great Britain, 1995

Nancy Barnett, Coordinator/Author, I CAN Work Program
Southside High School
1601 E. 26
Muncie, IN 47302

School telephone: (765) 747-5320
e-mail: nbarnett@cs.com

Awards: CEC Clarissa Hug National Teacher of the Year, 2000
CEC Indiana Teacher of the Year, 2000
State Farm Good Neighbor Award, 1999
Ellison Teaching Award, 1999

Debra Calvert, Eighth-Grade Teacher
John Hanson Middle School
12350 Vivian Adams Drive
Waldorf, MD 20646
School telephone: (301) 753-1783
e-mail: dcalvert@ccboe.com

Awards: Milken Family Foundation National Educator Award, 1999
Exemplary Employee of Charles County, 1998

Roy Coleman, Physics Teacher
Morgan Park High School
1744 W. Pryor Avenue
Chicago, IL 60643
School telephone: (773) 535-2550
e-mail: rcoleman@charlie.cns.iit.edu

Awards: Kohl Academy International Teaching Award, 1994
Tandy Technology Scholar National Award, 1994
Argonne National Laboratory, Sigma Xi Chapter, Outstanding
Physics Teacher, 1991

James Wade D'Acosta, Social Studies Teacher
Fairfield High School
Fitts House
755 Melville Avenue
Fairfield, CT 06432-2000
School telephone: (203) 255-8449
e-mail: jameswaded@aol.com

Awards: Harvard Teachers Prize, 2000: Awarded by the Harvard Club of Southern Connecticut for a faculty member "who inspires intellectual curiosity and the quest for excellence in students."

National Board Certification, 1999, in Adolescence and Young Adulthood/Social Studies-History: First in Connecticut and 1 of 106 nationally in my discipline and grade level. Refer to www.nbpts.org for information.

Celebration of Excellence Award by the Connecticut State Board of Education for American History Unit "Slaves, Masters, and Connecticut Yankees," 1997

William Ennis, Physics Teacher, Science Department, Chair
East Anchorage High School
4025 East Northern Lights Boulevard
Anchorage, AK 99508
School telephone: (907) 263-1297
e-mail: ennis_bill@msmail.asd.k12.ak.us

Awards: Milken Educator, 1999
Distinguished Teacher, White House Commission on Presidential Scholars, 1996
Alaska Teacher of the Year, 1996

Carmen Gumina, Biology Teacher
Webster High School
875 Ridge Road
Webster, NY 14580
School telephone: (716) 670-5000
e-mail: carm_gumina@ccmail.monroe.edu

Awards: Disney American Teacher Award, 1999
Wal-Mart Teacher of the Year, 1998
Webster PTSA Teacher of the Year, 1995

Linda E. Hains, Math/Science Program Coordinator
Rock Hill High School
320 West Springdale Road
Rock Hill, SC 29730
School telephone: (803) 981-1332
e-mail: lhains@rock-hill.k12.sc.us

Awards: State winner in the Technology and Learning Teacher of the Year program, sponsored by Microsoft, 1999
Honorable mention in the "National Technology Scholar Program," sponsored by Radio Shack, 1999
State winner in the Technology and Learning Teacher of the Year program, sponsored by Microsoft, 1998

Jenny W. Holmstrom, National Board Certified Math Teacher
Sumner High School
1707 Main Street
Sumner, WA 98390
School telephone: (253) 891-5500
e-mail: jenny_holmstrom@sumner.wednet.edu

Awards: First National Board Certified Math Teacher in the State of Washington, 1999
National Teacher Training Institute Teacher of the Year Award, 1998

Janine A. Jellander, Secondary Social Science Teacher
Mira Costa High School
701 South Peck Avenue
Manhattan Beach, CA 90266
School telephone: (310) 318-7337
e-mail: jjellander@manhattan.k12.ca.us

Award: Sallie Mae First Class Teacher of the Year, 1999

Carey Jenkins, Teacher, Basic Skills in English
President and Executive Director of Operation Link-Up
John F. Kennedy High School
61-127 Preakness Avenue
Paterson, NJ 07522
School telephone: (973) 881-6016

Awards: INROADS Frank C. Carr Community Service Award, 1999
New Jersey's Pride Award in Education, 1999
Reader's Digest American Hero in Education Award, 1998

Debbie Kelley, Family and Consumer Science Teacher/Teen Parent
Coordinator
New Direction Learning Center
Keller ISD
324 Keller Parkway
Keller, TX 76248
School telephone: (817) 337-3575
e-mail: DWH96@aol.com

Award: Secondary Teacher of the Year, KISD, 1999-2000

Rebecca Kelly, Special Education/Inclusion Teacher
Delmar Middle and High School
200 North 8th Street
Delmar, DE 19940
School telephone: (302) 846-9544
e-mail: rkelly@den.k12.de.us

Awards: International Reading Association, Presidential Awards for
Reading and Technology, 2000
Technology and Learning's Teacher of the Year State Winner,
Delaware, 1999
Project IDEA winner for "Working With WebQuests" from
Delaware Department of Education, 1999

Brenda Lynch, Spanish Teacher
Madison High School
800 Northeast 9th Street
Madison, SD 57042
School telephone: (605) 256-7706
e-mail: lynchb@madison.k12.sd.us

Awards: American Association of Teachers of Spanish and
Portuguese, 2000
Teacher of the Year for South Dakota, 2000
Technology and Learning Magazine, Teacher of the Year
Program, State Winner of South Dakota, 1999

Norma Butler May, Reading Specialist
Evanston Township High School
1600 Dodge Avenue
Evanston, IL 60202
School telephone: (847) 424-7400
e-mail: nbmay@earthlink.net

Awards: NAACP Image Award, 2000
Evanston Township High School, Evanston, IL, "Our School
Is Special Because of You," 1997
Kohl Academy International Teaching Award, 1994

Diana W. McDougal, Art Educator
Cheyenne East High School
2800 East Pershing Boulevard
Cheyenne, WY 82009-4294
School telephone: (307) 771-2663
e-mail: dmcdouga@wyoming.com

Awards: Wyoming Art Educator, 2000
National Art Education Association Marion Quin Dix National
Leadership Award, 2000

National Board of Professional Teaching Standards Certification, First Art Educator in Wyoming, 1999

Karla Mullen, English/Social Studies Teacher
Watertown High School
202 South Washington Street
Watertown, WI 53094
School telephone: (920) 262-7500
e-mail: mullen@execpc.com

Awards: Governor's Humanities Award for Excellence in K-12
Humanities Education, 2000
National Board Certification in Adolescent/Young Adult
Language Arts, 1999
The Wisconsin Council of Teachers of English Lucile S.
Pooley Award for Creative Teaching of English Language
Arts in Wisconsin, 1997
The Lawrence (University) Award for Outstanding
Teaching in Wisconsin, 1995

Shirley Newton, Science Teacher
Westerville North High School
950 County Line Road
Westerville, OH 43082
School telephone: (614) 895-6060
e-mail: newtons@westerville.k12.oh.us

Award: Ohio Technology and Learning Teacher of the Year, 1999

Debra D. Peppers, Vice President of Pepperseed, Inc.
1999 Retiree of Lindbergh High School
4900 South Lindbergh
St. Louis, MO 63126
School telephone: (314) 729-2400, ext. 1400
e-mail: drpeprs@aol.com

Awards: National Teachers Hall of Fame, 1999
Teacher of the Year, 1989
National Community Relations Award of Honor, 1991

Ronald W. Poplau, Instructor
Shawnee Mission Northwest High School
12701 West 67th Street
Shawnee, KS 66216
School telephone: (913) 993-7200
e-mail: ronpoplau@smsd.org

Awards: National Teachers Hall of Fame, 1999
Mid-America Education Hall of Fame, 1999
Kansas Legislature Citation, 1997

Nancy J. Pudas, Physical Education Teacher
Eden Prairie High School
17185 Valley View Road
Eden Prairie, MN 55346
School telephone: (952) 975-8230
e-mail: npudas@edenpr.k12.mn.us

Awards: Marie Berg Award, 2000
Disney American Teacher Award, Wellness and Sport
Category, 1999
Eden Prairie Secondary Teacher of the Year, 1995

Terrie Saunders, English Teacher, Department Chair
Omaha Central High School
124 North 20th Street
Omaha, NE 68102
School telephone: (402) 557-3300
e-mail: saundert@ops.org

Awards: Disney American Teacher Awards Honoree, 1999
Peter Kiewit Grant for Outstanding Teachers, 1998

Omaha Public Schools A+ Award for Creative and
Outstanding Teaching, 1997
Alice Buffett Outstanding Teacher Award, 1996

Robin Davidson Smith, English Department Leader/Teacher
Buckingham High School
Box 376
Buckingham, VA 23921
School telephone: (804) 969-6160
e-mail: ironrock@moonstar.com

Award: Virginia Teacher of the Year, 2000

Eileen Stewart, Teacher
Cypress Creek High School
1101 Bear Crossing Drive
Orlando, FL 32824
School telephone: (407) 852-3400
e-mail: steware@ocps.k12.fl.us

Awards: Tandy Outstanding Experienced Teacher, 2000
National Board Certified in Adolescent and Young Adults
Math, 1999
Air Force Association Outstanding Teacher, 1999

Wanda Jones Thomas, Teacher and Language Arts Department Chair
Nathan Hale High School
6960 East 21st Street
Tulsa, OK 74129
School telephone: (918) 831-7319
e-mail: thomawa@tulsaschools.org

Awards: Certificate of Excellence, Tulsa Public Schools, 2000
National Board Certified Teacher in Adolescent and Young
Adults English Language Arts, 1999
Teachers Touching Tomorrow, Tulsa Public Schools, 1998

I dedicate this publication to Joyce.

CHAPTER 1

Award-Winning Words of Wisdom

This is the place to read award-winning words of wisdom from your colleagues across the United States.

Chapter Overview

- **Jenny W. Holmstrom,** a national board certified math teacher at Sumner High School in Sumner, Washington, shares helpful hints developed over a 14-year career at the secondary level.

- **Carey Jenkins,** a teacher of basic skills in English and president and executive director of Operation Link-Up at John F. Kennedy High School in Paterson, New Jersey, asks and answers the question, "What is a good teacher?"

- **Ronald W. Poplau,** an instructor at Shawnee Mission Northwest High School in Shawnee, Kansas, says the key words are still what we learned very early in our own educational careers: "Experience is the best teacher!"

■ **Debra D. Peppers,** vice president of Pepperseed, Inc. and 1999 retiree of Lindbergh High School in St. Louis, Missouri, has come to the conclusion that preconceived stereotypes can be diminished, if not totally eliminated.

■ **Ronald W. Poplau,** an instructor at Shawnee Mission Northwest High School in Shawnee, Kansas, says that "goodness needs to be nurtured and never taken for granted."

▧ High School Teaching Tips

Jenny W. Holmstrom
Sumner, Washington

1. **Call home.** Somehow the practice of calling parents and keeping in touch with them stops when students leave the elementary grades. Granted, it is harder to call all the parents when faced with 150 students instead of one class of 30, but the benefits far outweigh the initial time invested. During the first two weeks of school, I call the parents of each student in each class. I call to introduce myself, tell them about the math program at the school, invite them to Open House, tell them about after-school math tutorial sessions at the school, and tell them how late I stay after school to provide extra help. The initial call sets the tone for the year and makes the students aware that I will contact their parents. Parents want to be involved and informed. Often, they are not given the opportunity at the secondary level.

2. **Reward good academics.** The main focus of school should be academic learning. I award a Math Student of the Month ribbon and certificate each month in each class. I hand out the ribbon and certificate and describe the traits that the student exhibited to win the

award. The traits vary from month to month. I prominently display the names of the winning students in my classroom. In addition, their names are posted in a window in the front office and in the parent newsletter. I also began the practice of sending home congratulatory postcards (they are provided by the school, embossed with the school logo) to parents of every student who earns an A on a math test. I do this all year long. Again, the time it takes to hand-write the postcards is worth the recognition the students get at home. Students value the postcards and save them from year to year. The parents appreciate the news because high school students generally neglect to share even good news at home.

    3. **Celebrate birthdays.** The first day of class I have my students fill out informational cards, and I always ask them to write their birthdate. I use this opportunity to explain the "Birthday Problem" and share the fact that if there are at least 23 people in the room, there is a very good chance that 2 have the same birthday. We check to verify the results. Then I explain that I will be writing all their birthdays on my desk calendar and that I expect them to provide treats for the class on their birthday. After all, why should the elementary classes have all the fun? Besides, this is the last time they will ever be asked to do so in their life! The students are always excited by the idea. I remind them when their time nears. After the first two provide treats, it becomes an established tradition. There are a few who can't or won't, and that is fine. I never make a big deal out of it. Most enjoy the treats and the opportunity to be recognized. The class community and goodwill generated by this small act last the whole year.

    4. **Involve parents.** I have made it my goal to involve the parents in each class at least once during the semester. I collected parent e-mails during Open House this year. With the increased use of computers and e-mail in the school and home, this is a great avenue for sharing information and giving feedback immediately. I have been planning one activity for each class I teach that requires that parents send something to school or come to school to help out with the task.

Again, the increased parent involvement and awareness show up in increased motivation and production in the classroom.

5. **Take risks.** Try something new. Go to a conference, and then try the latest ideas or techniques in your classroom. Students change every year. There are always improvements and new discoveries in the field. Make it your job to keep up with the changes and share them with your students. You will have fun, the students will have fun, and you will never tire of teaching your subject.

What Is a Good Teacher?

Carey Jenkins
Paterson, New Jersey

My teaching philosophy and practices evolved out of my experiences as a poor African American student growing up in rural Mississippi, where I attended elementary and high school. After high school, I attended California State University and graduated with a degree in business. I had a very successful business career with General Foods and Philip Morris Corporation. When I made the decision to leave industry and go into education, I wanted to teach and work in an inner-city environment with students who were from a socioeconomic background similar to mine. For me, the ideal place was the Paterson School District in Paterson, New Jersey, because I wanted to work with inner-city students who needed to be encouraged. I have received numerous local and national awards for my practices and results in the classroom. Among the awards I have received that are best known are the Reader's Digest American Hero in Education Award, received in 1998, and the New Jersey Pride Award in Education, received in 1999. Teachers must employ many basic and creative practices in the classroom to teach and to simultaneously instill in the minds of inner-city students the message that you are conveying the desire to learn.

My purpose here is to share with readers the seven approaches or practices that have always worked for me. The practices are as follows:

- A good teacher has to be a good salesman.

- A good teacher takes the child wherever he or she is and moves forward.

- A good teacher is a risk taker and disciplines with "tough love."

- A good teacher must motivate and build up the student's self-esteem.

- A good teacher must take a holistic approach in dealing with students.

- A good teacher must be able to control his or her students using the "tough love" approach.

- A good teacher must teach students the importance of education.

Selling Your Subject

A good teacher has to be a good salesman. If you can't sell, you can't teach. This philosophy applies to any classroom teacher in America, particularly in an inner-city environment. I have had many teachers in my life who have stood in front of the class and put me to sleep. The assumption teachers make when they stand in front of their class is that students know why they need that subject and why they come to school in the first place. These assumptions are totally false.

I started my business career after college as a sales representative for General Foods Corporation. When we went out to call on buyers each day, we did not make sales just by talking about our products. We had to talk about how the products we were selling would help the store. We had to explain how our products would make money for that store. Because we were often fighting competition, it was not always easy. However, we were getting paid to convince the buyers that they needed our products and that our products would generate a certain volume of business. That's what we called good salesmanship, and that is precisely what has to take place in the classroom. The math teacher must convince the students that they need math, and teachers of other subjects must do the same thing. If this selling process does not take place in the classroom, not a great deal of learning is going to take place. Clearly, this is what must take place in the inner-city classrooms across America.

Take the Child Wherever He or She Is and Move Forward

It was frustrating in the beginning because there were students who entered my class with different ability levels. Some students were at or above grade level, whereas others hardly knew what was going on. There were other students in my class who were highly motivated and others who did not know why they were in the class.

Many teachers placed in this situation start placing blame and making excuses for their anticipated failure by saying the following: These kids will never learn because they are from the projects, they come from deprived homes, or they were not adequately prepared in grammar school. Once you start doing that, you've lost the battle.

A teacher must take each student where he or she is and move forward. As a matter of practice, I start each class with a review of the material to be covered, followed by a pretest. By doing so, I know where each student is and can now proceed to teach. The teaching process takes place on a general level that is designed to reach the majority of the students. Small clusters of students who fall in front or behind the group are addressed individually. No one is embarrassed, and no one is singled out; it works each and every time.

A Good Teacher Is a Risk Taker

A good teacher will do anything that works to get the message to the students. I have known many teachers who use the same old lesson plans to teach the same subject year after year. If one approach does not work in a classroom, try another. A good teacher will experiment, try things, take chances, and do whatever it takes to give students good classroom experiences. In order to be effective in the classroom, a good teacher has to be a risk taker. To be effective, you must stick your neck out every day for your teaching philosophy and practices.

A Good Teacher Helps Students Believe in Themselves

In order to get African American and Latino youths to achieve, you must get them to believe in themselves. On a daily basis, African American and Latino youths are told that they are nothing and that they are nobodies in the home, school, and community. It is the first obstacle the classroom teacher must overcome if inner-city youths are to become good students.

Teaching them about their history can help African American and Latino students with their self-esteem. First, it should be noted that every group has its heroes, inventors, and achievers. Whether a teacher is teaching math, history, or science, approximately 10 to 15 minutes each period must be set aside to inspire, encourage, and motivate inner-city students. The class may be asked to research a prominent historical figure so that person can be discussed in class, or the teacher may simply select a prominent African American or Latino personality of the past or present and discuss his or her accomplishment with the students. This is one of several ways to get these students to feel good about themselves, which is the first step to instilling in them a desire to learn.

The majority of my students always did well because I told them they could do well. I told them they could do anything they wanted to do. I said this over and over again like a "broken record" every day. By the time they graduated, they believed it. What we are talking about again here is salesmanship. Our students (inner-city) suffer from low self-esteem. They tend not to believe in themselves because everyone beats them down. Once that confidence level is built up, the students are ready to learn.

A Good Teacher Deals With the Whole Child

When a teacher stands in front of an inner-city class, ready to teach, he or she is facing students with a variety of problems. Some of their problems are sufficiently serious that they take precedence over the subject the teacher would like to teach. An example of these problems may be physical, psychological, or sexual abuse. Other problems may be related to poverty, such as not having enough food, living in inadequate housing (crowded or not enough heat), or facing an eviction notice because of unpaid rent. These are everyday problems many of our students are dealing with. A good teacher will also make it a practice to get to know the parents of the students. It is not necessary to wait until Back-to-School Night to accomplish this. A phone call to the home or a note inviting parents into the school to visit the teacher or classroom of their sons and daughters is sufficient. Getting to know the parents accomplishes many things, two of which I will mention: (a) It enables you to understand the child better, and (b) the parent through this association becomes an ally rather than an enemy of the teacher. Having the parents of your students supporting you solves many problems with your students and administrators.

As a classroom teacher, I know that I have to deal with all the problems in these children's lives. I know that I am not going to teach students English, history, math, or anything else until I deal with whatever is on their minds. You are not going to be an effective teacher unless you take a holistic approach to teaching.

A Good Teacher Uses "Tough Love" to Control His or Her Students

I will talk about discipline because it is the biggest problem facing inner-city classroom teachers. The average teacher cannot control an inner-city class for several reasons: The teacher is afraid of the students and afraid of the parents of these students. In addition, teachers will say that they do not have the support of their administrators or that their administrators will not "back them up" when they attempt to discipline a child. I am by no means advocating insubordination, but the classroom teacher must be able to control his or her class with or without the backing of administrators. If this does not happen, no teaching will take place. My approach to classroom control was simple and direct: A child who did not follow the rules in my class had to leave class for that period and could not come back without his or her parents. Parents generally have jobs, other children, or other responsibilities and cannot afford to be running in and out of the school because of one unruly child. As a result, they (the parents) would force the child to behave so they did not have to come in every day. I call that parental involvement, and it works every time.

There are other reasons why there are so many discipline problems in the inner-city schools of the United States. Many of the teachers have no respect for these students. The students are very much aware of this lack of respect, and they show it. In addition, the teachers have very little respect for parents as well, and the parents are equally aware of this lack of respect. An excellent classroom practice is to show respect to your students and their parents. You have to give respect to get respect. It works. Trust me.

When I was in the classroom, I referred to my students as Mr. Smith or Miss Jones (pseudonyms) when I addressed them. When possible, I greeted my students at the door when they walked into the classroom. I stood at the exit door and said good-bye, shook every student's hand, and said "Have a nice day" at the end of class. My students learned early that I respected, loved, and understood them. They also learned early on that I am in control of my classroom.

Teaching the Importance of an Education

I can remember that during my preteen and teen years, I would sit in class daydreaming, wondering why I needed to learn algebra, history, science, and so forth. Many days, I wondered why I needed to be in school at all, particularly since I thought I knew how to read, write, and do arithmetic. Most teachers assume students come to class each day knowing why they are there. In fact, students come to school knowing not much more than that one needs an education to better his or her life. That simply does not tell students enough.

Students have to be taught why they go to school and why they need to study math, social studies, science, and so forth. My approach to this is simple and highly effective. Here are two strategies that could be used to stress the importance of education:

1. Bring professional people into the school to talk about their lives and careers. Students are able to learn from these individuals what they do and what academic preparation is needed to do it. By listening to these professionals and asking questions about all the little nuances of their jobs, not only do students learn what they like or dislike about careers, they also learn what preparation is needed in the academic community to go into a career and excel in that career. In these meetings, students learn why math is important to the engineer or why biology or chemistry is important to the premed student, and so forth.

2. Take students out into the marketplace to visit plants, factories, corporate offices, military bases, and so forth. The reason for this approach is to enable students to see firsthand what goes on in these institutions. In addition to observing what goes on in general, our students are invited to "shadow" certain people to get a firsthand, close-up look at certain careers. Also, it is hoped that students will see others of their own race on these experiences, which provides a collateral benefit that helps build self-esteem.

Once students recognize all the academic subjects needed to get a degree in a particular field, they are more prone to study, stay focused, stay in school, and do all the things necessary to learn, get a diploma or degree, and accomplish whatever goals they set out to accomplish.

Another very important advantage of visiting institutions and having people come to talk about their lives and careers is that students learn how and where these people live. Students learn what these people are able to do with salaries of $50,000 to $100,000 per year. The point made here is that these students learn what they must do in order to emulate the highly successful people they have observed and heard speak in their classrooms. One speaker or corporate visit per month is sufficient.

All of my adult life I have heard teachers and others talk about why learning does not take place in the classroom (particularly in inner-city classrooms). Let me share with you some of the reasons given by teachers for poor classroom performance: oversized classes, inadequate facilities, no computers, poor teacher salaries, discipline problems, and children not coming to school ready to learn. I feel that every teacher should assume some responsibility for the students' failure to learn. If learning is not taking place, we must look at ourselves first. If we teach students to believe in themselves and to understand the importance of an education, and if we get our classrooms under control, more learning will take place. In addition, the teacher, to be effective, must take a holistic approach in dealing with students in an effort to get his or her message across in the classroom. There is no magic associated with any of these practices. Nor does one have to be a renowned scholar or Ph.D. to implement or employ these practices. It is all really common sense. Think about it.

🔖 Student Creativity

Ronald W. Poplau
Shawnee, Kansas

All my life I have been an avowed enemy of what I call "Read and Recite, Tell and Test." I actually cringe at the sight of students copying from textbooks to hand in as a study guide. We know only too well that assignment results in a committee of students who take turns doing busywork.

Although my subject is sociology, this approach or philosophy crosses all disciplines. The key words are still what we learned very early in our own educational careers: "Experience is the best teacher!"

We need less repetition and more creation. Sociology is really a contemporary subject that tries to make some pattern or reason out of today's numerous events. The textbook lists up to 10 different kinds of studies sociologists can employ to make social data meaningful. At the *informational* level, these 10 ways really have little if any meaning—they are something for students to organize, memorize, and quickly forget once the examination is over. At the *creative* level, however, they take on a whole new life of their own. In the classroom, students were assigned to create an original sociological study based on any of the 10. Not surprisingly, the most popular studies centered around a *planned* study wherein the budding sociologist had to "cause" something to happen. The next most popular study was the *participatory* study, in which the students themselves were an integral part of the study. Here are examples of student creativity that is meaningful, creative, and downright fun.

Case 1

Where would you expect people to get involved if an injustice were taking place before them? This site was hypothesized to be a church. To prove this assertion, the student made confidential arrangements with the minister to steal the collection plate *during the Sunday service.* "Theft Sunday" found numerous student "worshippers" who wanted to see what would happen. To our dismay, only shocked glances and frightened worshippers were evident as the student left the church immediately following her row's donation.

Another Sunday, a different church in a different city brought almost identical results. However, there was one new twist to this study: One of the worshippers called the school to complain about this method of instruction. She soon hung up during a cross-examination that resulted in self-incrimination for not "getting involved."

Case 2

Are homosexual marriages accepted? Under usual classroom conditions, a few homophobic students would respond with a disgusted

"NO," leaving the remainder of the hour to the all too common, "I don't know!" Two young men and two young women (high school seniors) thought of a new method to test for acceptance. They went to various jewelry stores to buy wedding rings for an "intended gay marriage." With the assistance of confederates throughout each store, they discovered latent homophobia and outright prejudice. One salesperson, a woman, cautioned the young female "lovers" to be careful, saying she ought to know, as she was gay herself! The discussion that followed in the classroom crossed multiple chapters, and needless to say, "let me try this one" was the most common remark from a room full of students.

Other Creative Cases

Students came alive with a keen desire to find some method to study social phenomena. One student asked the question "Are humans gullible?" To find out, he wondered if they would buy invisible fish with the promise that they would materialize in two weeks? Gallons of empty water were sold! Another wondered if anyone would stop a thief in a local store. How about two young men who asked for donations in a pail so they could buy drugs? Thirty minutes in a shopping center netted them a little over $15! Students took grandparents to bridal shops for obvious age differences in nuptials. Little kids five or six years of age smoked fake "cigarettes" and drank fake "beer" in public, only to learn that no one cared.

Perhaps the most meaningful study involved Christmas cards from someone who never existed but which were sent to real friends and relatives. The instructor provided the use of his home address. Nearly 50% responded, and one even suggested a holiday get-together that involved a special dinner. A phone call from the fictitious person resulted in an invitation for dinner, and the person never asked WHO HE WAS. How far humans will go to simply save face!!

Strange as this might seem, I really had no intention of being a teacher, but I accepted an invitation from a principal who saw something in me that I did not see in myself. As might be expected, I was failing miserably in the classroom and to my rescue came an English teacher, with a "planned study" of her own. She told me to ask my students a simple question: "Why are we not getting along?" At first, I was more than a bit angry at her intrusion in my class, but upon reflection I thought, "Just what I should have known all along: LET US DO SOMETHING!" My students taught me what no education class up to then did: EXPERIENCE IS THE BEST TEACHER!

Last summer I was inducted into the National Teachers Hall of Fame, with a subsequent induction into the Mid-America Education Hall of Fame. To my surprise, many former students wrote from all over the country. Their most important question was, DID I REMEMBER THEIR SOCIOLOGICAL STUDY?! My former history students remembered the history pageants, the reenactments of great historical figures in their most significant roles. Thirty-eight years later, and it was still with them!

There is a textbook in my room, and the students all have one, but they no longer bring them to class. I find it significant that my students scored highest on any district criterion reference test. We have long since required additional teachers for sociology. We all work together, and I see creativity growing. Recently, I was taken to the superintendent's office on some outrageous charge, only to learn that it was a sociological study. The kid got an A+.

Helpful Tips

1. The District will buy you textbooks. It is nice to check them out and have the students find something in the book that you are covering. Our district just bought sociology books at $45 each.

2. Have the students fill out a complete plan on what they are going to do. Also have them list WHEN and WHERE. A student sent out 140 racist letters without my knowledge or approval. The Federal Bureau of Investigation; postal inspectors; channels 4,

5, and 9; and all the local newspapers were after me. It turned out wonderfully!

3. There are so many things the teacher can do to judge the abilities, maturity, and so forth of his students. I had a woman come who faked statistics and said she was forming a Parents for American Education group. It was unbelievable how much our students need critical thinking.

4. Students love to share their studies because they are *theirs*. Let them judge first-, second-, and third-place winners.

5. Do one study together: We did the Christmas Card Study, and it was the life of the class.

🢒 Breaking Stereotypes Through Interactive Role Playing

Debra D. Peppers
St. Louis, Missouri

Desegregation is not integration. My great-grandmother, a full-blooded Chickasaw American Indian, passed down the adage "Walk a mile in my moccasins." By literally placing oneself in "another's shoes" through simulated role playing, I have come to the conclusion that preconceived stereotypes can be diminished, if not totally eliminated. After three years of experiential classroom learning, culminating in three successful student-oriented programs, this past year was spent evaluating the effects of each for analysis in an ongoing action research project.

Raised in a small integrated town in northern Missouri, I then experienced prejudice and hatred at the University of Alabama in the late 1960s. After a frightening semester of student teaching at Theodore, Alabama, during its first year of forced integration, I became aware of the impending need for change. My entire teaching career has been in the predominantly white Lindbergh School District in St. Louis County, and only after court-mandated busing in 1979 did my African American students begin to see changes in curriculum.

My first experience with the effectiveness of role playing began with a student returning to a theater class after six weeks in a drug rehabilitation center. The students were so eager to hear all that "Curt" had experienced that many began to share their own problems, including racial prejudice and the effects of being stereotyped. We developed a one-act play from the acted-out scenarios, and the results were more than dramatic. Our student audiences were personally affected, and many sought counseling for their own problems. After several articles in local newspapers, Southwestern Bell Telephone hired me for the summer as an educational consultant and made a video and teachers' packet the following fall. My students and I were able to reach schools throughout a six-state area. *CHOICES,* as we called it, won a St. Louis Emmy award for educational broadcasting in 1989.

The second ongoing program incorporating role playing began in a partnership program with Sumner High School in St. Louis, Missouri, four years ago. KSDK channel 5 provides the expertise in writing, producing, and role playing in public service announcements; we provide the students. Our aired topics have included gang violence, staying in school, racial prejudice, child abuse, and teen suicide.

The third and final project was through the Voluntary Interdistrict Coordinating Council's (VICC) search for 10 committed teachers, 5 black and 5 white. After volunteering summer hours to work together to share ideas and talents, we each came up with individual programs that would be scheduled in school districts throughout the St. Louis area. My project was originally titled "A World of Difference" but was later confused with another local program of the same name; therefore my program was retitled. "Unique Begins With You" involves students of mine accompanying me and performing for Grades K-12 throughout the area. After researching "not-so-famous African Americans who still left their mark," we role-play through the use of simple skits, song, dance, and game-show format for assemblies of several hundred students.

The focus of this year's action research was to document—through ongoing journal entries, video and audiotape, and professional input—to what degree the role playing actually affected the lessening of prejudice and stereotyping. My personal bias predicted that the results would be overwhelmingly in support of my opinion. What I had not anticipated was the most troubled, violent, unpredicted turbulence in the history of our school. I kept an ongoing collage of the articles and clippings of a student walk-out over a controversial black speaker, stabbings, weapons confiscated, assault, and numerous suspensions. The focus of my research could no longer be limited to the confines of my classroom or programs; I now for the first time realized the necessity to strive to affect the entire student population and ideally to expand community- and citywide.

After documenting the predominantly supportive results of the journals and cumulative questionnaire results of the participants, I then documented the lesser, but significant, negative input by those seemingly unaffected. I focused on two vignettes of individual students: one a very successful, enthusiastic black sophomore male; the second a negative, self-admittedly prejudiced senior white female. Both were very open, honest, and cooperative in sharing their viewpoints, family backgrounds, and progress. Both *did* show varying degrees of improvement. The questionnaires were then distributed to all my students who had been in each class experiencing the role playing, whether they had participated in the three projects or not. Summaries were related but rather inconclusive because of the unexpected events of the year.

The strengths of the role playing in each of the programs as well as in the overall outcome were reflected in the responses of the students. As noted in sample quotations, the vast majority of all students related that the role playing enabled them to see the various situations from a different perspective and gave them new insight into the perceived as well as the real prejudices. In addition, they reflected that the nature of the classes themselves and the enthusiasm and support of the teacher made them more open to the role playing itself. They felt they had ownership in the project, security to express their true feelings, and freedom to explore solutions in a nonjudgmental setting. An increasingly large number of students expressed a desire to become involved in the classes as well as the varying programs.

On the other hand, the weaknesses of the programs were reflected this year more than in the last three years because of the volatile year we experienced. There were honestly more feelings of prejudice expressed; more violent confrontations arose; and less input was seen on a schoolwide basis. The frustration level of those involved in the different programs was increased because of the fact that the publicity and news coverage reflected only the negative within our school district. All of us worked even harder to "spread the word" about the positive activities we were doing.

As the year came to an end, it eventually paid off. Every school in which we had performed sent us letters of thanks and encouragement to continue the programs. We were recognized by VICC Headquarters, the St. Louis Partnership Program, KSDK channel 5, and St. Louis *Post Dispatch*; most recently, I have been named one of the recipients of the World of Difference Awards for advancing positive human relations.

The summation of this year's research culminated in the conclusion that, overall, each of the three programs using the role playing should be not only continued but expanded. Careful attention must be given to those selected for advancing these projects. Not only are the contents of the sources themselves important, but there are three crucial criteria for expansion: (a) The first demand is that there be a strong, caring, emotionally involved teacher who believes in the necessity of the program. (b) Students must be involved on an interest and volunteer basis and must be encouraged to explore at their own pace and level. (c) As much administrative and professional input as possible should be explored. The extension possibilities for similar programs in the community are endless.

The overall conclusion validated my threefold purpose: The year of observation, evaluation, and reflection indeed confirmed the need for this project; the three years spent in implementing and improving these programs has been substantial; and the direction and potential future needs of each project are clear. Involvement of more students, parents, faculty, administrators, and professionals in education and business can all be incorporated in expanding these programs to have an even larger impact.

▧ The Doer of Good Becomes Good

Ronald W. Poplau
Shawnee, Kansas

It is unfortunate that Columbine High School has changed the reputation of our young people. All the stereotypes of "sex, drugs, and violence" are, after all, true, and we must change our schools to prevent such a disaster from ever taking place again! Fortunately, Columbine is merely an aberration—tragic but in no way typical of today's young people.

At Shawnee Mission Northwest High School just the opposite has been true since the day it opened in 1969. The students have collected food, clothing, and even presents for all the men at the state prison. In 1991, we decided to make this an autonomous class. It was eventually called "Cougars Community Commitment." It is a social science offering for a half-credit per semester. It is open to juniors and seniors, and with approval of the sponsor, students may enroll for as many as four semesters.

Seventeen students were enrolled the first year, and those 17 set a standard few classes have met. Few in the community took the class seriously: Rake the lawn, mow my grass at no charge?! Our class motto was simply "THE DOER OF GOOD BECOMES GOOD!" It was and is our opinion that what we used to take for granted now has to be taught. Goodness needs to be nurtured but never taken for granted.

I remember our first major project: saving a couple's home from foreclosure. The wife had spina bifida and had a hospital bill of $40,000. They appealed to us for help. Those 17 students took on the couple's plight as if it were their own. They invented "Dollar Day" at the high school, petitioned local businesses for donations, and accumulated enough to refinance the couple's home and even reduce their monthly house payment. With $2,700, they worked a modern-day miracle. The wife, in tears, thanked the entire student body, who responded with a standing ovation and a "let's do it again" chant. The rest is history.

The CCC (as it is commonly called) has grown to include half the junior and senior classes. It is a voting member of the city government of the City of Shawnee. The program now comprises five classes a day, with an agenda that simply staggers the imagination, including a monthly dinner dance for the elderly held in the school cafeteria on the final Saturday of each month. Students begin decorating at 2:30 in the afternoon. By 4 p.m. guests start arriving, and a dinner is served by the students at 5:30, with dancing to a live orchestra. Students and the elderly dance together, dine together, and, above all, mingle with each other. This mutual intergenerational experience benefits both age groups.

Other projects have included taking care of a couple's pet dogs while the husband was in a local hospital. Two girls and a delivery man put up an entire new ceiling for his homecoming because the fine dust from the ceiling would have affected his emphysema. When he died unexpectedly, eight CCC girls carried him to his final resting place as pallbearers.

Students raise all the monies themselves by a variety of projects: coupons at a food store, dues, Dollar Day, and donations. The budget tops $10,000 a year. They help the elderly pay for ambulance service, pay utility bills of the indigent, and rebuild homes and lives after fires. This past year they provided Thanksgiving dinner for over 500 families. Truckloads of food left our school as students boxed and delivered the holiday meal.

Their charity is not limited to the traditional poor but was also extended to an ex-convict who had spent 54 years in prison. That criminal had the dubious honor of being what the Kansas Secretary of Corrections said was "undoubtedly the most dangerous and cunning criminal to ever occupy a cell in the 110-year history of the Kansas State Prison." In addition to giving him the necessities of life, the students also became his good friend and frequently socialize with him. The convict's recent book bears this inscription: "DEDICATION TO MY FRIENDS AT SHAWNEE MISSION NORTHWEST HIGH SCHOOL, RON POPLAU AND THE KIDS OF CCC. THEIR HELP MADE MY TRANSITION TO THE COMMUNITY EASY."

Along the same lines, the CCC students gave each of the boys and girls at Associated Youth Services a generous Christmas present of a basketball, a Walkman, a T-shirt, and a sweatshirt. In utter surprise and with a voice full of emotion, one boy shouted, "I don't want to hear anyone say anything bad about S. M. Northwest, or they will have me to answer to!"

The lives of the CCC students have been drastically changed as well. One student gave up drugs, remained in school, and even became a speaker for graduation. She went on to college and is now happily married. Her parents give the CCC an average of $1,000 a year in gratitude. Another student won't go to the district's Alternative Placement Program because they do not have a volunteer program. Forty-five students tutor at elementary and middle schools every day. Test scores have risen from almost all Ds to not lower than a B. Individual students reward their classes with pizza parties, cookies, and movie tickets.

Once a month, Lakeview Retirement Village sends a delegation to our school for the monthly dinner with the students in our cafeteria. White tablecloths cover the tables, flowers and candles provide fitting decorations, and students sing during the meal. An 88-year-old woman took the microphone to thank the students, only to break down and cry; in tears she said, "We love you all!"

Needless to say, these students have not gone unnoticed by civic groups in the area. It would be impossible to list all the awards these students have won: Penney's Golden Rule Award four times; the SERTOMA award; Noxema Kansas Award; Prudential, Kiwanis, and Optimist Awards. In addition, *Kansas City Star* ran a special on the class; a doctoral dissertation on this type of education was written on them; and just a month ago they were the guests of the governor of Kansas in the State Capitol building for the Governor's Spirit of Giving Award.

Last year, I was inducted into the National Teachers Hall of Fame as a result of the work these students do on a daily basis. No fewer than 15 awards have been directly given to me, but none will top the parting gift from last year's CCC. They all gathered at the front office and formed a kind of gauntlet. Amidst cheers, applause, and tears, they presented me with a tuxedo for the Washington, D.C., induction ceremonies. In the pocket was a card signed by each member with the words "KNOCK 'EM DEAD IN WASHINGTON, D.C."

What a shame, what an injustice that these students get overlooked by the media and people in general for the trenchcoat mafia and two crazed students at Columbine High School. Judging by the number of visitors and inquiries, *this* program is reaching more and more high school students. A Kansas legislator will introduce a bill to make this program mandatory in each high school in Kansas. Many years ago, the great educator and president of the United States Woodrow Wilson said, "Nothing but what you volunteer has the essence of life, the springs of pleasure in it. These are the things you do because you want to do them, the things that your spirit has chosen for its satisfaction." At Northwest High School we simply say "THE DOER OF GOOD BECOMES GOOD!"

Helpful Tips

1. Start small and let one success build on another.

2. My enrollment for next year is simply out of control—I will have almost 500 students.

3. I have sample contracts for each student—I would be glad to share these with anyone interested.

4. The district and the high school just love this class. It costs them nothing, and the publicity is beyond words.

5. Self-esteem skyrockets. Anyone can be successful in this class. I am not surprised that the most common grade is an "A." That represents 65 hours per quarter of volunteer work.

6. Guest speakers every now and then help a great deal.

7. Last Thanksgiving, the four volunteer classes fed 500 families a complete meal.

8. Many students enroll for four semesters. This class is only open to juniors and seniors because members must be able to drive a car.

CHAPTER 2

Succeeding With Reading and Writing Instruction

T his chapter shows how other high school educators are teaching reading and writing.

🔖 Chapter Overview

■ **Norma Butler May,** a reading specialist at Evanston Township High School in Evanston, Illinois, says that "in today's classrooms, one can advocate the graphic organizer as a strategy to make learning more meaningful and a delight to secondary students."

- **Terrie Saunders,** an English teacher and department chair at Omaha Central High School in Omaha, Nebraska, has her students study the heroic characters found in many works, including *Idylls of the King, Ivanhoe,* and *Silas Marner.*

- **Robin Davidson Smith,** an English department leader/teacher at Buckingham High School in Buckingham, Virginia, says that students enjoy reading primary resources that are "real" and that give a good feel for the culture.

- **Terrie Saunders,** an English teacher and department chair at Omaha Central High School in Omaha, Nebraska, has her students participate in this newspaper project. She says it develops writing skills, provides an outlet for creativity, and develops an understanding of the importance of teamwork.

- **Wanda Jones Thomas,** teacher and Language Arts Department Chair at Nathan Hale High School in Tulsa, Oklahoma, offers an innovative way to teach Shakespeare's *Hamlet,* featuring group presentations.

- **Jean E. (Keppel) Baldikoski,** an English teacher at Naperville Central High School in Naperville, Illinois, says that evaluation can take many forms. "Since most of my students take many forms, and since most of my students have considerable experience with the literary essay, I use performance assessment as the means to determine whether these honor students have mastered the content of this weighted literature course."

- **Debra Calvert,** an eighth-grade teacher at John Hanson Middle School in Waldorf, Maryland, uses reading logs for many reasons, including encouraging reading outside the classroom.

- **Terrie Saunders,** an English teacher and department chair at Omaha Central High School in Omaha, Nebraska, has her students complete an independent reading project requiring students to read a book, write a paper, and give a speech.

■ **Wanda Jones Thomas**, teacher and Language Arts Department Chair at Nathan Hale High School in Tulsa, Oklahoma, created a unit enabling her students to immerse themselves in the culture of Asian peoples.

■ **Wanda Jones Thomas**, teacher and Language Arts Department Chair at Nathan Hale High School in Tulsa, Oklahoma, explores Asian literature with her students. She says this "unit gives the students a cursory overview of a people who deserve our admiration and our thanks for the many aspects of civilization they have shared with the world."

Graphic Organizers and Their Enhancement of Reading Comprehension on the Secondary Level

Norma Butler May
Evanston, Illinois

In the 18th century, many secondary teachers were searching for new ideas or strategies to help improve reading comprehension in their reading or content area classes. In today's classrooms, one can advocate the graphic organizer (which uses visual representations of how ideas are related to each other) as a strategy to make learning more meaningful and a delight for secondary students. The graphic organizer can make information more apparent, distinct, and articulate for the learner. Since its first introduction, the graphic organizer has undergone many changes in definition and style (Elan, 1999).

I taught the novel *Taking Sides* by Gary Soto, an award-winning author of numerous books for adults and young readers, which takes as its central theme ethnicity in America. This touchingly realistic story explores the divided loyalties of a Hispanic basketball player, Lincoln, who has recently moved from a poor neighborhood to a more affluent one. Soto masterfully conveys the Hispanic American experience. Several graphic organizers were used in teaching this novel.

Students were allowed to go to the computer lab and use selected *Internet sites* to look up Gary Soto's life history and review other novels that he had written. The following day, the students reported back to the class on the information they had found.

Before students read the book, I introduced the **Word Knowledge Rating Scale** (Blachowicz, 1986), which is a prereading activity designed to introduce a list of potentially unknown content words to students. The Word Knowledge Rating Scale uses a survey format to have students determine their knowledge of a word or concept. As students surveyed and participated in class discussions, they became aware of how much they already knew about the subject to which the words were related. The students checked the words they could define, those they knew something about, and those they didn't know at all. The words used on the Word Knowledge Chart were *ethnic, adolescence, Hispanic, barrio, Chicano, emotions, vignettes, struggle, neighborhood,* and *characteristics.*

Next, the **Anticipation Guide** (Herber, 1978) was used. This is a strategy that forecasts the major ideas of a passage through the use of statements that activate students' thoughts and opinions. Before reading the selection, students responded to several statements that challenged or supported their preconceived ideas related to key concepts in the novel. Students then had an opportunity to explain or elaborate upon their responses in a small group.

Concept Definition Mapping (Schwartz & Raphael, 1985) is a graphic structure that focuses students' attention on the key components of a definition: the class or category, properties or characteristics, and illustrations or examples. The key word presented helped the students understand the meaning of the word *affluent,* because Lincoln had moved to a more upscale neighborhood. The students worked in pairs. When they finished, the category of the word was given, and some of its characteristics and examples were shared. Other vocabulary words were also used.

The **Analogy Graphic Organizer** (Buehl, 1990, as cited in Buehl, 1995) was a strategy used to provide a visual framework for the students to analyze key relationships in an analogy. The compare-contrast structure served to broaden their understanding of important concepts by comparing Lincoln's old neighborhood to his new one. In addition, this organizer was used to compare and contrast Lincoln's new school to his old school.

After each chapter was read, the class did an **Intensity Scale,** in which they filled in the graph-scale based on the story's events. Thirteen events were listed in sequential order, and students shaded in the intensity of each event with a 1-to-10 rating scale, in which 1 indicated low intensity and 10 indicated extreme intensity. The students enjoyed using the colored pencils to highlight the intensity, and this served as a good review of the novel.

The **Venn Diagram** (Clarke, Martell, & Wiley, 1994, as cited in Lenski, Wham, & Johns, 1999) was used to compare and contrast the main character, Lincoln, with the character Tony. I modeled this strategy using the class's input to determine what is the same about these two characters in the book and also what is unique to each of them. Two overlapping circles were drawn: Characteristics shared by the two characters were written in the shared area, and in each of the circle areas outside the shared space, characteristics unique to each character were rerecorded.

Upon the completion of reading the novel a **Story Pyramid** (Waldo, 1994, as cited in Lenski et al. 1999) was used. This activity helped students reflect on and organize their responses to the novel. Students thought of words that described the character, setting, and events from the novel they had read. Words were asked to be inserted for eight statements:

1. Name of the main character

2. Two words describing main character

3. Three words describing setting

4. Four words stating problem

5. Five words describing one event

6. Six words describing second event

7. Seven words describing third event

8. Eight words stating solution

After the students had completed of reading the novel, they were given a student reflection handout to describe the graphic organizer that helped them the most.

Helpful Tips

1. The teacher should model the use of the organizer before asking students to use the organizers independently. You may use an overhead transparency, a drawing on the blackboard, or a large wall chart.

2. Class participation to generate ideas on how to use a graphic organizer and cooperative groups proved to be successful in reinforcing its use.

3. Positive attitudes toward reading can be developed through the creativity of using graphic organizers.

4. Encourage students to construct their own graphic organizers.

5. Graphic organizers can be used as another means of assessment.

Standards: Comprehension

6. Use questions and predictions to guide reading across related materials.

7. Explain and justify an interpretation of a text.

8. Interpret, evaluate, and apply information from a variety of resources to other situations (e.g., academic, vocational, technical, personal.)

9. Summarize and make generalizations regarding the effectiveness of the author's intent.

10. Analyze how authors and illustrators use text and art to express and emphasize their ideas (e.g., imagery, multiple points of view, artistic elements).

Standards: Vocabulary

11. Compare the meaning of words and phrases, and use analogies to explain the relationships among them.

12. Analyze the meaning of abstract concepts and the effects of particular word and phrase choices to comprehend and to expand vocabulary.

References

Blachowicz, C. (1986). Making connections: Alternatives to the vocabulary notebook. *Journal of Reading, 29,* 643-649.

Buehl, D. (1995). *Classroom strategies for interactive learning.* Schofield: Wisconsin State Reading Association.

Elan, M. (1999). Reselections on effective use of graphic organizers. *Journal of Adolescent and Adult Literacy, 42,* 641-645.

Lenski, S., Wham, M. A., & Johns, J. L. (1999). *Reading and learning strategies for middle and high school students.* Dubuque, IA: Kendall/Hunt.

Herber, H. (1978). *Teaching reading in the content areas* (2nd ed.). Englewood Cliffs, NJ: Prentice Hall.

Schwartz, R., & Raphael, T. (1985). Concept of definition: A key to improving students' vocabulary. *The Reading Teacher, 39,* 676-682.

Further Reading

Allen, J. (1999). *Words, words, words.* York, ME: Stenhouse.

Billmeyer, R. (1996). *Teaching reading in the content areas: If not me, then who?* Aurora, CO: Merel.

Dennis, M., Green, P., Levine, G., & Troy, A. (1999). *Graphic organizer collection.* San Antonio, TX: Novel Units.

Johns, J., & Lenski, S. D. (1997). *Improving reading: A handbook of strategies.* Dubuque, IA: Kendall/Hunt.

Tarasoff, M. (1994). *Reading instruction that makes sense.* Victoria, British Columbia, Canada: Active Learning Institute.

Vacca, R., & Vacca, J. I. (1999). *Content area reading.* Reading, MA: Longman.

▧ The Hero in Literature and in Life

Terrie Saunders
Omaha, Nebraska

The sophomore English curriculum that I teach focuses on a study of literary heroes. Over the course of the year, my students study the heroic characters found in *Idylls of the King, Ivanhoe, Silas Marner, The Old Man and the Sea, A Tale of Two Cities, Julius Caesar,* and *Othello* as well as Greek and Roman mythology. However, students often have difficulty making the concept of heroism meaningful to their own lives. This unit on heroes provides a focus on heroism—not just in the fictionalized view of literature but in students' own lives.

My approach is threefold. We discuss first a literary model, then a historical model, and finally a personal/contemporary model. Although I have used this approach with several different units of study, *Idylls of the King* works especially well for me because I begin the school year with this work, and I can then build on the discussion of heroes through the remainder of the school year.

To introduce the unit, I use an audiotape to initiate discussion. In the past I have used Simon and Garfunkel's "Mrs. Robinson" and have handed out the song lyrics for discussion. We focus on the lines "Where have you gone, Joe DiMaggio? The nation turns its lonely eyes to you." (I particularly like using these lyrics because my second unit is *The Old Man and the Sea,* a novel in which Joe DiMaggio is a heroic figure to the main character, Santiago.) Other songs, such as Tina Turner's "We Don't Need Another Hero," work just as well to stimulate a discussion on heroism.

The discussion of the song lyrics sets the tone for the unit and leads into the discussion of the literary hero King Arthur from Tennyson's *Idylls of the King.* Over the next several weeks the class studies Tennyson's idylls, focusing on such matters as the qualities that lead to Arthur's rise to power, the perfection of Arthur's kingdom, his impact on his knights, Lancelot's contrast with Arthur's goodness, and Arthur's disillusionment. Although the unit of study incorporates a variety of literary topics, from allegory to scansion to figurative language, the focus always comes back to Arthur's heroic qualities as they are similar to or different from the qualities of other characters in the work.

While the class involves itself in the discussion of King Arthur, students work on several independent projects. I ask students to keep a scrapbook of newspaper or magazine articles related to different people or situations that they feel reflect heroism. They clip the article, identify the source and date of publication, write a brief summary, and identify heroic qualities. Sometimes, I ask students to keep the scrapbook during one unit only. At other times, I have them keep the scrapbook throughout the school year to use as an overview of the year of heroes.

Students also research a figure from history who has been identified as a hero in some way. While allowing students to continue their study of heroes, the research element also provides a review and practice of research techniques. Through the research, students must identify the person, provide background information and details about the person's life, and identify his or her heroic qualities. I encourage the selection of often overlooked figures, especially minority figures and women. I provide some suggestions (especially of little-known figures) and have a list of possibilities available, although students are not restricted to using my suggestions. A day in the library with the assistance of the librarian helps. The librarian can guide students in their selections and, in my school anyway, can provide a lesson on Internet research.

Students then present an outline of their research, provide a bibliography with at least five sources, and complete a three- to five-minute speech that has a visual or audio aid—a time line, a poster, and so forth. Some years I have required a written research paper with endnotes and works cited page. Other years I have required only the formal outline and bibliography. The speech substitutes for the written paper. I prefer to have my students give a speech, as they need this type of presentation practice more than they need the research format.

The final activity is a return to the original song by Simon and Garfunkel and the original question, "Where have you gone, Joe DiMaggio?" I ask students to reflect on whether there are still heroes and who they are. This introduces the third aspect of the unit—the personal/contemporary model. This comes at the end of the unit, after the discussion of King Arthur and after the research project and speeches. In many ways, it is the culminating aspect of the unit. (Sometimes I use this at the end of the school year—after the study of numerous literary heroes.) Students write an essay discussing a hero of a more contemporary nature—someone they know or someone they have read about in the newspaper (the scrapbook is helpful here). They write the essay explaining who the person is and why he or she is a hero in the view of the student-writer.

Either at the end of the unit or at the end of the school year, students present their scrapbooks. Often, I request that students include as part of the scrapbook an interview with an adult regarding a personal hero from his or her era. The interview is submitted in a question-and-answer form. Some students turn in videotapes or audiotapes along with the transcribed interview.

This unit can be easily modified to meet the needs of the students and curriculum. The advantage of having so many elements in the unit is that it accommodates a variety of student interests and ability levels. Those students who are comfortable with public speaking have an outlet, as do those students who prefer quiet library research. By requiring all students to complete each aspect of the project, the unit gives all students experience with writing, research, and public speaking, but it does not focus so heavily on one aspect that the student's grade is dependent on his or her success in that one area.

Along with providing students with the opportunity to continue their development of previously acquired skills in reading, writing, speech, research, and technology, this unit also provides an opportunity to incorporate multicultural elements as well as interdisciplinary contact. Over the years I have modified the unit—actually, I modify it yearly based on the nature of the students in my classes—but overall it has been successful in terms of student achievement.

Helpful Tips

1. When I require students to complete an interview, they often need guidance in selecting the person whom they should interview.

2. I provide minideadlines along the way to be sure students are working on the project and not waiting until the last minute.

3. This is a very flexible project. Some elements can be adjusted to work with other units or omitted as time constraints affect the schedule.

4. It is necessary to plan ahead. I work with the librarian and the computer lab staff. Knowing ahead of time what I am asking students to do, the librarian or computer lab staff can often provide a brief lesson on research and Internet use.

5. I grade each element of the project separately. I provide students with numerous handouts explaining in detail my expectations and the basis of my grading.

Using Primary Resources for Literature Units in Secondary English

Robin Davidson Smith
Buckingham, Virginia

Have you ever wondered what the penalty was in Anglo-Saxon England for stealing a nun or grabbing her by the breast? Or what the legal situation was for an Anglo-Saxon man who remarried after his first wife had been kidnapped by the Vikings, only to have her turn up again 10 years later? Or what the punishment was for throwing up in church after taking communion—or worse, having the dogs in church lick up the vomitus? Or why the fine for cutting a man's beard against his will was greater than the fine for cutting his hair? Or why the fine for killing one man might be greater than the fine for killing another man, but both fines would be less than that for killing any woman? If you are like my students, you can't help but be intrigued by these questions once they are posed, and I take full advantage of that curiosity.

I usually teach English 11 and 12, including reading, research, literature, and composition. The literature selections for English 11 and 12 center around the American and British literary canons, respectively. English teachers are both blessed and cursed with an infinite variety of materials to work with and skills to work on—skills that don't necessarily have to be taught in a certain sequential order. Because making these constant and myriad choices is so time-consuming, it is very tempting simply to cover literature in the chronological order of the test, pausing briefly to introduce historical background before beginning a new literary period and stopping occasionally for an essay or research project. However, this practice is generally stultifying for students and frustrating for teachers. It also encourages students in their tendency to see everything they learn as a discrete bit of knowledge, unrelated to anything else in their experience.

Most literature written before the mid-20th century is on a college reading level or beyond, so a constant diet of it for months on end does little to stimulate interest or improve reading proficiency. Students get little exposure to technical reading, which requires its own skills. Even after such a chronological survey of literature, few students seem to have any grasp of the history or of how the pieces fit within the development of the culture. The assigned writing tends to be consistently literary. Using this strictly chronological survey of literature causes all sorts of problems in the secondary classroom, fails to address real student needs, and does not utilize students' innate curiosity. The approach that works best for me is units that combine a variety of reading, speaking, research, and writing experiences gathered around a common theme or topic. I cover the canon in essentially chronological order, but I include primary source material (such as "The Laws of King Alfred," the source for the questions with which I began this discussion), contemporary parallel technical and literary reading, and technical writing in each unit. Of course, doing the necessary research means more work, but it's worth it.

For example, I begin the Anglo-Saxon period by posing these questions, which center the unit and which we revisit periodically:

- What is a man? What qualities should a man have?

- How does a society encourage a male to become a certain type of man? Why?

- What happens to men who don't meet their societies' expectations?

- Do the answers to these questions vary from culture to culture? Why?

We do the usual small-group and large-group brainstorming and reporting. We may tape a sign listing a quality on the back of each student and have team captains collect students with the qualities they most need in a specific situation. Students may bring in news articles about men, which we dissect for the qualities displayed by the subject. We then categorize the characteristics as being attractive in a date, a father, an employee, a soldier, a driver, and so forth. Through the entire process, students keep ongoing notes of the "manly" qualities, how they're demonstrated, and social consequences for having or not having the appropriate characteristics.

Once I am convinced that everyone has considered these questions in a more than superficial manner, I get students to skim "The Laws of King Alfred" and "The Laws of Edward and Guthrum" (Attenborough, 1922). (This is also useful for introducing Old English, for the Old English version is on the left-hand page and a modern translation is on the right.) This reading activity is directed. They must answer questions such as the following:

1. Based on the severity of the penalties, what did the Anglo-Saxons consider the worst and least offensive crimes?

2. Who received the fines paid for crimes against women? Why?

3. What evidence do you find that the Anglo-Saxons were Christianized?

4. What evidence do you find that the Anglo-Saxons were still superstitious pagans?

5. What is *wergeld/wergild?* (Figure it out from the context.)

6. How were fines for crimes against a particular person determined?

7. Who was responsible for paying the fines? Why?

8. Under what conditions were people imprisoned?

9. What were relations like between the Vikings (Danes) and Anglo-Saxons? Why?

10. What laws did they have that we don't? Why?

11. In what ways is our legal system different?

12. Which law is the most bizarre?

Students are always pointing out notable laws to their neighbors and exclaiming loudly while they skim this. Some always beg to take a copy home. I refuse, because I time it so that they don't get their fill before class is over. I want them to rush into class the next day ready to tear into those texts again. I take up their notes before they leave. Their responses give me an idea of how carefully they've read and what they are thinking.

I begin class the next day with small-group discussions; they have to produce one answer for each question with specific references to a particular law. This refreshes their memories and forces them to go to the text. Then the entire class tries to come to consensus after each group reports. We revisit the "man" questions.

Students then go back into small groups to answer two questions, which will lead to research: What do we need to know about these people (the Anglo-Saxons and the Vikings) to understand them? What do we want to know about these people? Students also must skim the Anglo-Saxon background section in several literature texts for ideas. We divide the topics, discuss possible sources, and make sure that everything significant is covered. A student is in charge of organizing this; I just throw in suggestions as necessary. I make sure that some things are covered, such as having one pair do the term *blood-feud* and read "The Wife's Lament" and "The Husband's Message," two Anglo-Saxon lyric poems that revolve around blood feuds. In addition, each group is responsible for finding a contemporary article to print for the entire class to read. The article must relate to one of the topics people in the group are researching, must be interesting to the class (other students grade each group on the interest and relevancy of its article), and can be no longer than 500 words (must be cut if it's longer). When I stipulate that it must be related, I use the term loosely. For example, a group with a student researching Anglo-Saxon folk remedies might include magazine articles about any of these topics: recipes for love potions, a witches' coven suing the city of San Francisco, current research showing the scientific basis of folk remedies, or a chemical analysis of physical attraction.

I always insist on both print and nonprint sources for research and a formal works cited or works consulted list. Students' reports are both oral and written, and I usually have them practice oral reports for their groups before they perform in front of the whole class. The group also checks any written work because students get an individual grade as well as a group grade. Before the presentations, each group must design a note-taking guide for the rest of the class with major headings and numbered spaces underneath. This helps students develop organizational and note-taking skills. The written format varies (definition, encyclopedia entry, outline, advertisement, message in the personals column), but because this is usually one of their first written assignments, and I'm usually working on clarity and conciseness, I limit it to 50 to 100 words. I usually insist on one graphic. We use PowerPoint if we can get in the computer lab and if I can schedule the projector or LCD to use with my laptop. Otherwise, students do professional-looking displays with my large felt board and my shelves. (I am lucky to be in a renovated library with a wall of shelves.)

We usually do one group's presentations a day because students can listen attentively and critically for only so long. Students listen, take notes, evaluate individuals, read the chosen article silently, have small-group discussions of the article, and then evaluate the group using the rubrics given out before students began their research. Keep the rubrics simple but specific. You don't want students to spend 20 minutes figuring complicated mathematical formulas, but you also don't want them giving everyone "A"s—even those who did not make eye contact, who read from notes, or who had a confusing note outline—just because they're nice, lazy, or ignorant of what is demanded. The first few times I have students evaluate others I grade them on the accuracy of their evaluations to force them to be honest and critical—in the true sense of the word.

After we've finished all of this, students read the historical background section on the Anglo-Saxon period. It is surprising how much more of it soaks in when they have prior knowledge to which to attach the information. Then we read Beowulf; I always read it aloud as a directed listening-thinking activity. (For example, what evidence is there that the scribe who recorded *Beowulf* was a Christian? Or, according to these lines, how big is Grendel?) Most students don't visualize when they read silently or orally, and they read in an uninflected monotone. They visualize when I force them to stop and respond in writing or by drawing. Students often get ticked off at my continuous interruptions, but that's good: It means they are curious enough to be anxious to get to the next part. Often, I'll assign each student a sentence or two to practice reading orally after I have read that section aloud. The students reread it aloud after I have heard them privately and corrected their inflection. Of course, we reread only the juiciest parts—never things like lists of gifts or armor (which I tend to skip myself, only commenting that the next 50 lines list all the gifts that Hrothgar gave to Beowulf in gratitude for his services). Before we finish with *Beowulf,* we revisit the "man" questions and students add to their lists.

I usually round off this part of the unit by having students do some sort of project. They are warned to be thinking about this in advance. I accept anything: diary entries, songs, posters, T-shirts, models, dioramas, monsters, games—whatever plays to the student's strengths. The class establishes guidelines for what is necessary for a specific grade: Not all projects are of comparable complexity and value. After students show their projects to the class and explain what gave them the idea and what problems they had with execution, I read short excerpts from two variations on the Beowulf story, John Gardner's *Grendel* (1976) and Michael Crichton's *Eaters of the Dead* (1989), and encourage students to read them in their entirety for extra credit. Since *The Thirteenth Warrior* was released (a movie version of *Eaters of the Dead*), we watch it and do a 250- to 500-word literary comparison. This first literary paper is usually done in groups, and I assign very limited topics. Students are aware of their topics before we watch the movie, so they can take notes as we watch. I stop the film periodically so that they can compare notes and clear up any problems; otherwise, writing about a film becomes very difficult. Also, I put names and bibliographical information on the board before we start to reduce confusion.

Once we finish *Beowulf,* we usually read a number of excerpts from Bede's *Ecclesiastical History of the English-Speaking Peoples.* It's full of great stories that are culturally revealing and that clearly trace the changes in what was needed/expected of a man as England became Christianized. We also read excerpts from the penitential manuals used by priests to standardize the punishments for different sins. They are as entertaining as Alfred's laws and just as culturally revealing. The culmination of this unit is designing the perfect contemporary American man. Each individual designs one, and then groups form a composite if they can come to consensus. The design includes an illustration. These become quite elaborate sometimes:

One group had a flip chart that allowed the viewer to substitute different heads (each with its own mental strengths and attitudes), different hearts (showing various emotional makeups), and different bodies (demonstrating a myriad of physical attributes).

Students enjoy reading primary resources, which are "real" and give a good feel for the culture. Students then see the fiction as something created by and for specific people and can test their own beliefs against something concrete. The use of contemporary nonfiction also helps in developing readers and thinkers who can make more connections and be more thoughtful and critical. Even juniors and seniors still enjoy doing projects. Working together forces them to teach each other, to verbalize more clearly, and to rethink ideas—and to enjoy doing it. Moreover, with the class organized like this, students feel more in control of their learning even as I steer them through a series of specific experiences.

How This Fits the Virginia Standards of Learning

The Virginia Standards of Learning End-of-Course Tests for the secondary level are administered in the 8th and 11th grades. The Reading, Research, and Literature Test for junior English includes specific questions on the American literature classics but also requires that students be familiar with many other types of reading. Many English teachers find it difficult to incorporate technical and nonfiction reading in their courses; this approach prepares students for the reading on the test and ensures that they remember much more of the classics that they have read. Doing small research projects continuously rather than just one large research paper exposes students to a variety of sources and reinforces sound research techniques. The oral presentations help them retain information and also ensure that students do have instruction in formal speaking, which is one of the untested standards often ignored. The writing-to-learn as well as the formal writing projects assist students with the Writing Test as well. This method is a review without the boredom associated with review.

Helpful Tips

1. I learned more in the first year I taught than in the 16 years I had been taught in school. Unfortunately, it took me almost another 16 years to come to the next logical conclusion: If I want students to really learn, I should put them in situations where they can and will teach themselves and each other rather than my trying to cram it down their throats. When I teach, I learn. When they teach, they learn.

2. Unless something is totally fascinating and entertaining, I can't sit still and listen for more than 20 minutes. I have much more patience and am interested in many more things than the average adolescent. Ergo, if I talk to a class for more than 20 minutes at a time, I deserve any inattention and behavioral problems I get. Anything that requires more than 20 minutes of teacher-talk should be explored in some other format or broken down into smaller segments.

3. Search the Internet for materials, ideas, and sources. Bookmark them for yourself and your students. Almost every university has wonderful English sources online (e.g., the University of Virginia's English Department has a site where you can read and hear Old English pronounced accurately). Using e-text versions makes access easy. You don't have to spend hours holed up in a library to find wonderful things in the public domain.

4. Get evaluation textbooks from every publisher on the planet. They are invaluable as sources for you and your students. One textbook will not give you everything you need. Some will have detailed background and author material; another will contain contemporary fiction and multicultural literature to use as parallel reading; and others will have exciting primary source material. (Who could resist the newspaper account printed in Coleridge's time about a ship that was becalmed with penguins packed in brine that oozed huge worms that ate

the very planks of the ship?) Most will have lists of further reading.

5. Read constantly yourself—not just fiction but also magazines. You will find material that will relate to what you're doing in class and will fascinate your students.

6. Ask your librarian for help in finding additional reading and for advice on avoiding copyright infractions.

7. Spend more time on planning than you do on grading. Remember that the goal of education is learning, not evaluating.

8. Find ways to reduce your grading. (And when you do, call me!) Although writing groups do work, I still believe that students also need constant feedback from a professional—the teacher. That does not mean you have to take home a stack of papers every night. Walk around the room, skim, make comments, and have students write down your suggestions. Grade just one question or paragraph; you can usually identify the crucial piece that will tell you what the student knows or can do. Evaluate or respond rather than grade; make students see that all learning is a process. Provide rubrics for everything; they ensure that students understand your expectations and make grading quicker for you. A well-designed rubric for a specific task can be used over and over. Model for and train your students in evaluating themselves and others. We had to learn how to look and what to look for, and so do they. Find ways to make students responsible for evaluating themselves and others. It's the best way to learn.

9. Assume that you will make at least five mistakes a day and that you don't know everything. Your students will have a lot more respect for you if you accept that fact with grace and humor. Set up situations where you are the student and they are the teachers.

10. Watch your tone and train your students to be aware of their own tones. No one learns in a classroom with a bad atmosphere.

11. Ask questions rather than making accusations.

12. Make sure that your students know they are your primary concern and you care about them as individuals. It's amazing how much work they will crank out and how much easier they will make your life if they know you care.

13. Have fun. Teaching English offers you more intellectual freedom and more scope for variety and creativity than any other job in the universe. If you aren't enjoying teaching, it's a bad personality/age group fit, or your focus and methods are wrong. Find someone on your staff who seems to really enjoy teaching and ask for suggestions. If that doesn't work, get out. You can make a lot more money doing something else that is better suited to your personality.

References

Attenborough, F. L. (1922). *The laws of the earliest English kings.* Cambridge, UK: Cambridge University Press.

Crichton, M. (1989). *Eaters of the dead.* New York: Vintage/Random House.

Gardner, J. (1976). *Grendel.* New York: Ballantine.

The Newspaper and the Novel

Terrie Saunders
Omaha, Nebraska

This newspaper project can be used with a variety of units. I have used it with *Idylls of the King, Ivanhoe, Julius Caesar, A Tale of Two Cities,* and *Othello.* It provides a review of the unit itself, develops writing skills, provides an outlet for creativity, and develops an understanding of the importance of teamwork.

At the point when the class is nearing the end of the unit, we spend one day discussing the local newspaper. I bring in copies of the newspaper and ask students to locate different types of articles that I list for them. (Sometimes, I give them a list of types of articles and ask students to bring in samples of each as a homework assignment.) We discuss the ways in which the articles reflect the era and the society in which we live. Students then discuss what constitutes each type of article. Students who have taken a journalism class immediately become class leaders.

I then give the class a handout explaining the project. They are asked to create a newspaper based on the novel the class is reading. For example, if I do this project with the *A Tale of Two Cities* unit, students create a newspaper from the era of the French Revolution. In their newspaper, they must include certain types of articles that I designate—such as feature stories, national news, obituaries, editorials, and so forth. They may add other elements as they see fit—advice to the lovelorn, cartoons, want ads. The content of the articles must relate to characters, events, and locations from the novel. The newspaper must be text based.

I tell students that they will work in groups of three to five students. They may select their own teammates. Before I ask students to determine the students with whom they want to work, we spend time discussing teamwork with a handout that identifies some ideas to think about before choosing partners. I remind them of the problems often faced in working with partners and explain to them that they are to make wise selections. Part of the project is to work together to create a finished product. I advise them to select teammates who can provide what the group will need to complete the project—workers, artists, leaders.

If they select someone who does not do much work, then the understanding is that this has been a conscious choice made so that others can complete the paper in their own way. I remind them that friends do not always work well together. They will not have much in-class time, so they will need a common study hall or predetermined times when they can get together at school or outside school as is necessary. I tell them that once they have their groups in place, if a problem arises, my response will be "Just fix it." I give students several days to think about their groups. Then I take the names of the students on the team and the name they have given their team.

I require students to assign specific tasks to group members. They must set up a work schedule and provide me with their work schedule deadlines. They keep logs identifying the time they have spent on the project either alone or with the group. Because I provide very little in-class time, they need to work outside the class. I keep my room open before and after school on a regular basis so groups have somewhere to meet and work. Although I do not require that the finished product be word processed, I do make available the use of the computers in my room and in the building because most students want to turn in a computer-generated finished product. In many cases, students have computers at home, and often groups select a student to be part of the group because he or she is comfortable on the computer or has access to a computer at home.

At some point early in the project, we discuss the criteria for grading. Students need to know early what the expectations are. Students provide ideas on what they think should be considered for grading purposes. Usually, they consider elements of creativity, overall appearance, and depth and accuracy of content to be the major considerations. I ask them to clarify each of the broad topics. For example, creativity might mean the use of graphics, color, additional stories not required, and so forth. From their responses I provide a handout that identifies for students the guidelines that they themselves have determined. I also tell them that they will be responsible for grading each other's newspapers.

After the teams have finished their newspapers, students show the class their work and read a few of their articles. With the completed project, students must submit their individual logs, and the team must submit a sheet identifying the individual responsibilities of each student. Students then have several days to come in and look over the papers.

During one class period, students have a second opportunity to view the displayed newspapers and complete an evaluation form based on the criteria that students discussed earlier in the project. The newspapers themselves have a number assigned to them so that student names do not appear. (Sometimes, I have a different class complete the evaluation.) I then add my input before computing the final grade for the project.

Students have enjoyed this unit. Because of their involvement with both the creation of the project and the grading, they seem to feel as though they have more control over the outcome. They also seem to want to please their peers—or maybe it is the competition with their peers that they desire. Whichever it is, the newspapers offer an interesting and creative review of the unit.

Helpful Tips

I try to determine my grading criteria before discussing grading with the class. In this way I can guide students in the direction I want them to go. Even though I warn students about careful selection of teammates, I still have to step in and solve various problems. Although I try to tell them to "just fix it," sometimes they do not have enough experience with problem-solving and people skills to correct the problem. At that point, I step in and try to offer some suggestions.

▨ Succeeding With Reading and Writing Instruction Integrating Technology: A Study of *Hamlet* From Pit to Stage

Wanda Jones Thomas
Tulsa, Oklahoma

The study of Shakespeare's *Hamlet* opens so many doors for learning that one has simply to choose which direction and which purpose. This unit serves many areas of education in a high school English class. The goals for this lesson are for students to know Hamlet's story, including the milieu in which Shakespeare wrote this play, and also to know something of the audience who judged this dramatic presentation. Students will need to know the material well enough to present, know how to write and to speak about their ideas, and then be able to communicate their part of a team effort to keep the team strong. Several steps lead to the exciting conclusion of this unit.

1. *Monday.* When students enter the room, they find from five to seven posters placed on the bulletin boards. Each poster is identified with one or more of these topics: royalty, medicine, the arts (e.g., music, painting, architecture), laws, government, travel, commerce, housing, or science. Subjects are chosen by interests of the students, and if three or four students suggest a subject not offered, the new one is added. Students then sign the poster for the subject chosen, and groups are formed by the students themselves. My rationale is that students work better in areas of interest and when they feel comfortable with each other.

2. Each student receives an assignment sheet, and about 15 to 20 minutes is allowed for group discussion as students plan what they need for the presentation. The whole class then spends the remainder of the 90-minute class period working in the library.

3. *Tuesday.* Students are given 20 to 30 minutes to organize their material, to decide parts for each person in the group, and to plan the presentation. The rest of the class period is spent together as a class discussing the introductory material to the play and reading the play aloud in parts. Having different volunteers each day for role playing gives everyone a chance to be heard. The players either stand in the front of the class or move their chairs onto a pretend stage at the front so that every person in the audience can see and hear the performances. We use the Folger's Library paperback version of Hamlet's story with explanations on the left page. Students are free to interpret their parts with feeling, movements, and facial expressions. At the end of each scene, the audience asks questions of the actors about "why or how or whether"—whatever will help to understand the scene.

4. *Wednesday.* Some time is allowed for group consultation. I visit with those in each group to discuss their progress. I want to know if they will be ready to present the next day and whether there is anything they need that I can do or provide. Technological aids need to be ready for use, and if this use means making arrangements with the technology supervisor, the students must do this for themselves. In the room, they already have a few items, including a computer, television, overhead projector, and AverKey, but a PowerPoint projector or other machines must be brought in by the students. For the rest of the period, we continue to read the play aloud.

5. *Thursday.* Group presentations take the whole period. As each group presents, the rest of the students evaluate the material and techniques and assign grades to the group and to individual members on a sheet prepared by me. These sheets are turned in before the class leaves the room. By assigning small groups to study the background material, I am able to get students involved in finding facts, doing research, and working together in teams. Their discoveries enrich the main goal of learning Hamlet's story by their finding peripheral information and by my empowering students to take charge of a portion of their own education.

When we finish reading the play, discussions center on the question of whether a person is in control of his or her life or is destined to certain fates from which there is no escape. Students have a round-table discussion, with the chairs in a circle if space allows. Discussion begins with a clean sheet of paper on each desk and with each student writing a response to the question. Then each student must find three examples in the story to support the response. With this hard copy of their thoughts unsullied by others' ideas, the discussion begins with the question, "What were Hamlet's options?" Other questions include the following: Why did Gertrude marry so soon? Would Hamlet have been a good king? By comparing other sons who lost fathers (Fortinbras and Laertes) to Hamlet, what does the reader learn about the character of the Prince of Denmark?

The unit ends with an essay of five to seven paragraphs, answering the question about fate and how a person's character traits or habits seem to point toward certain kinds of fates. The students are expected to use other stories (perhaps Oedipus or movie characters) to compare or contrast with Hamlet. However, if an advanced thinker has a better idea, I gladly make exceptions for the essay subject. For the homework assignment, the students have three days to write, to polish, and to hand in the essay about Hamlet.

Helpful Tips

My first time using this method was fraught with frustrations. Perhaps I can save others the stress. I expected each person to be in class when his or her group presented. Of course, every teacher has those students who insist on failing and will not cooperate. To keep from penalizing the group if a member was absent, I added the requirement that any absentee must present his or her own materials with his or her handouts, visuals, and everything. Being absent meant the absentee had to begin anew and bring a new product, not a warmed-over version of what the group had already presented. Attendance has improved on the day of presentations, and I like to believe lessons learned are not only about Elizabethan England and a prince but also about our habits and attitudes and how we program ourselves for success or failure.

The next year when presentations were made, I invited a neighboring teacher to bring her students in as part of the audience. Her class, which was studying several Shakespearean dramas, proved to be a worthy audience in that they knew something about the material and judged the researched products, the performances, and the visual aids from a rather educated viewpoint without feeling pressure to give "A"s to all students. Classmates who were waiting their turns to present tended to give higher grades, hoping they would receive higher grades in return from friends. The visiting class teased the presenters, in some cases, about the power they had been given, and a few tried good-naturedly to barter for reciprocal good deeds. My students were encouraged to do their best because the other class was seen as a real audience. I interpreted this tendency to show off as the other side of taking pride in doing good work. Generally, the presentations won the audience's interest, spoke to the matter eloquently, and provided information that enriched the audience's understanding of other works by Shakespeare. In a class last year, I watched with pride as some students mentioned *Romeo and Juliet* and *Macbeth,* aspects of which were illuminated by their research. They had studied Romeo's story three years earlier, when they were freshmen, and Macbeth's story the previous year. As seniors they gained new insights as unexpected rewards for their hard work.

In the spirit of Teachers Touching Tomorrow, I experienced one of those heart-filling moments when two young ladies told me they enjoyed this unit so much that they finalized their decisions to become teachers and to attend my alma mater, Oklahoma Baptist University. They saw the possibilities for enlarging their own worlds through the interchange of ideas, and they formed new friendships as they worked with people of like interests in preparing their reports. Grouping by interest instead of by proximity in the classroom affords students the freedom of expression through acceptance into a new group; encourages creativity as the team members bounce ideas off each other; sets up a need for technological skills found in a few individuals; and brings out individual talents to prepare the written, spoken, or visual elements. I have overheard remarks of students praising each other for the parts each added to the team effort. How students can be in class with each other for 18 weeks and not know everyone has always been a mystery. This project overcomes the anonymity and enables the class to become a group of friends, or at least acquaintances. Of course, I haven't established Utopia, but the assignment appeals to multiple intelligences and talents. Part of my reward as a teacher is in seeing students who are usually reticent actually being drawn into the group activities. A sullen young man, an aspiring rock group drummer, became a major player in his group when he was asked to use his drums in the musical accompaniment to the presentation. He received applause, increased self-esteem, and even money (when he sold a few of his band's CDs).

One team, whose subject was royalty, made their presentation on PowerPoint as a form of *Jeopardy,* a favorite game show. One student asked the questions, and another sat at the computer to signal frame changes as he and the rest of the group were contestants answering the questions. A picture of Queen Elizabeth I ended the presentation. Looking at the picture, I knew something did not seem right. I was puzzling over the difference until suddenly I recognized the Queen's face as my own. When I exclaimed, "Oh, that's my face," the whole class, who knew before my epiphany, had a good laugh on me when I did not even recognize my own picture set in the resplendent headdress and royal costume of the Queen. The group had scanned my yearbook picture and inserted it into the PowerPoint frame. We all had a good laugh, and the presenting team received all "A"s when the grades were assigned by their peers. Of course, I also thought they were extremely precocious and creative.

State Standards

Many of the standards of Priority Academic Student Skills (PASS) are fulfilled in the unit. The relevant standards are listed in the following:

I. *Reading process.* A. Vocabulary. 1. Continue to build personal vocabulary through word study, the reading of literature, and class discussion. 3. Use word meanings within the appropriate context, and verify those meanings by definition, restatement, example, comparison, and contrast. 4. Connect technical and specialized terms with new concepts in content area text.

I. B. *Comprehension.* 1. Read and comprehend both fiction and nonfiction that is appropriately designed for grade-level reading. 2. Preview the material and determine the purpose for reading a specific text. 3. Use prior knowledge to become actively engaged with the reading material, and use a range of comprehension skills (e.g., literal, inferential, and evaluative). 4. Skim text for an overall impression, and scan text for particular information. 7. Vary reading speed and strategies according to the type of material and the purpose for reading.

I. C. *Fluency.* 1. Increase reading speed and comprehension through daily independent reading. 2. Continue to read with expression, interjecting a sense of feeling, anticipation, or characterization.

II. *Responding to text.* D. Evaluate works of world literature as reflections of time and culture. I. Use knowledge of literary genre and text structures to aid comprehension (drama, poetry, short stories, essays, speeches, and novels). K. Analyze details for relevancy and accuracy. P. Evaluate, react, and respond to reading material through activities such as discussions, correspondence, family histories, Reader's Theater, and multimedia projects.

III. *Information and research.* A. Use clear research questions and suitable research methods (e.g., library, electronic media, and personal interview) to elicit and present evidence from primary and secondary sources. C. Give credit for both quoted and paraphrased information in a bibliography. F. Select the best source for a given purpose (e.g., reference books, almanacs, atlases, encyclopedias, dictionaries, thesauruses, electronic card catalogs and databases, tables of contents, glossaries, indexes, magazines, newspapers, and *Reader's Guide to Periodical Literature*). H. Develop and organize notes from content area text using graphic organizers, note cards, or outlines. I. Use supplementary resources to enhance understanding of content area subjects (e.g., audio or video recordings, print materials, and interviews). J. Analyze, synthesize, evaluate, summarize, and paraphrase information from multiple sources.

IV. *Effective reading habits.* D. Read for a variety of purposes, such as for pleasure, to gain information, to communicate, or to support an opinion.

VI. *Grammar/usage and mechanics.* A. Demonstrate appropriate practices in speaking and writing. Students are expected to write using complete sentences and to edit for usage, mechanics, and spelling. B. Demonstrate correct use of standard English.

VII. *Listening/speaking.* A. Demonstrate thinking skills in listening, speaking, reading, and writing. For example, students, individually or in groups, will gather information, organize and analyze it, and generate a report that conveys ideas clearly and that relates to the background and interest of the audience. B. Prepare, organize, and deliver oral responses to literary works. 1. Summarize significant events and details. D. Present reports using appropriate delivery (volume, rate, enunciation, and movement) and language skills (pronunciation, word choice, and usage). E. Analyze purpose, audience, and occasion to choose effective verbal and nonverbal strategies such as pitch and tone of voice, posture, and eye contact. J. Evaluate the spoken message in terms of content, credibility, and delivery. K. Show consideration and respect for others. 2. Speak responsibly to present accurate, truthful, and ethical messages.

VIII. *Visual literacy.* A. Distinguish fact, opinion, and fiction in print and nonprint media, such as literature, electronic media, and advertising. E. Access information from a variety of media (television, computers, videos, CD-ROMs), and evaluate the quality of the material selected.

IX. *Literature.* B. Demonstrate a knowledge of literary elements and techniques and how they affect the development of a literary work. For example, students are expected to recognize and explain plot, character, setting, theme, conflict, symbolism, point of view, imagery, flashback, foreshadowing, irony, tone, and illusion. D. Read and respond to historically or culturally significant works of literature. For example, students are expected to find ways to clarify the ideas and make connections between literary works. E. Expand vocabulary through word study, literature, and class discussion. F. Draw inferences such as conclusions or generalizations, and support them with text evidence and personal experience. G. Recognize and discuss universal themes (archetypal patterns) in literature. I. Analyze, evaluate, and explain the thinking or behavior represented in a work of literature from or about various past and/or present cultures and relate it to own culture.

UNIT
Hamlet, Prince of Denmark by William Shakespeare, 1601

TEXTS

The Elizabethan theater. (1993). In *World literature.* Austin, TX: Holt, Rinehart & Winston.

Shakespeare, W. (1992). *The tragedy of Hamlet, prince of Denmark.* New York: Washington Square Press.

PURPOSES

    A. To know the story of *Hamlet*

    B. To study the elements of literary tragedy and tragic families

    C. To find reasons why Shakespeare is considered a great writer

        1. Poetry

        2. Psychology

        3. Humor

        4. Figurative language

    D. To learn the milieu out of which Shakespeare created the play

        1. Philosophy

        2. Royal family

        3. Historical facts: travel, housing, government

        4. Fine arts: drama, art, or music

        5. Science or medicine

CLASS ACTIVITY

    1. Work in groups and present information to the class (Homework #1).

    2. Each group will have 15 minutes on Tuesday, _____.

HOMEWORK

    1. Each student will pick one of the areas of inquiry regarding the milieu and come to class with notes and documentation of information. Register your choice with me.

2. Memorize the "To be or not to be" soliloquy for recitation to me or to the class.

3. Read the handout about the play, and write at least 10 questions you would like to have answered during the study of this famous drama. These questions are due as you enter the classroom on Monday, _____.
These will be returned Tuesday.

4. Keep a journal of the story. Set it up as shown here. Following instructions and being neat are part of the grade for this assignment. Due Friday, _____.

Shakespeare
1. "Has this thing appeared again?" (I.i.28)

My response
Fearful that the ghost is a devil and not Hamlet Sr., they call it a "thing." (A)

Shakespeare
2. "the morn in russet mantle clad" (I.i.181)

My response
Beautiful imagery of the sun's rising on a new day. (C)

GUIDELINES FOR THE JOURNAL

1. Make neat columns. Draw a line to separate columns if you need to do so.

2. Number the entries. You must have at least 15 entries.

3. Each of your responses will be tied to one of the purposes for which we are reading the play. My first example is "A," to

learn the story, and the second is an example of "C," figurative language.

4. Leave a space between entries so that I know which response goes with which entry.

5. Identify the line of the play by putting the number in parentheses following the quote.

6. Bring the journal to class each day.

Performance Assessment: Mixed Media in a Literature Class

Jean E. (Keppel) Baldikoski
Naperville, Illinois

The students crowded into the practice room, some spilling out into the corridor, eager looks on their faces as they anticipated the start of Lauren and Courtney's piano and flute duet. But before they began to play, the girls explained that they wanted to portray romance and tragedy, two universal literary patterns, through "the world's language, music." Lauren proudly proclaimed, "If a picture is worth a thousand words, then I believe that a musical composition is worth a thousand pictures." These two young women were poised to present their final examination in an advanced placement literature course titled "Romance and Tragedy."

Evaluation can take many forms, and because most of my students have considerable experience with the literary essay, I use performance assessment as the means to determine whether these junior and senior honors students have mastered the content of this weighted literature course. About three weeks before the end of the term, I offer them a variety of opportunities to demonstrate that they understand and can apply the concepts of the course. Suggesting as many as seven options, I also encourage them to propose their own means of showing their mastery. Lauren and Courtney chose to create a musical composition, one of the exam possibilities I offered.

In their duet, Lauren and Courtney contrasted the archetypal garden and the hero's quest of the romance story with the tragic hero and corrupted garden of the tragedy story. Choosing a flute to represent man, they early on established him as the focal point around which the rest of the piece centered, with their initial melody—simple, sweet, and in a major key—depicting man's innocence. They used the piano to symbolize all of the outside forces that affect man, its notes initially harmonizing with the original melody. In order for the man to be in perfect harmony, he must change himself to adjust to the garden, and to show this adjustment, the musicians slightly altered the original melody. Eventually, failing to preserve harmony, man leaves the garden, and the piano descends into a minor key, indicating that he is crossing the threshold into the wasteland where the hero's journey begins.

The musicians depicted the wasteland in a minor key; a mournful, solitary, changed man traverses this section alone, scared and unsure of what will come. Inevitably, when he battles against a monster, the composers shifted the piano part into a bass clef. The bass line speeds up, becoming frantic as the hero and the evil fight. Eventually the hero wins, and the song swings gloriously back into a major key.

All seems to be going well for the man, but a new disturbing element enters his newfound peace in the form of a serpent, a menacing figure that casts the man out of his garden and into a strange world; here, the music lapses into a minor key. Thus, the tragedy section begins, with the music of the tragic hero's journey paralleling his enigma, his indecision, and his downward spiral, showing the folly of his choice.

To illustrate the chaos of the next section, the students played clashing chords that grated on the audience's nerves. Here, the flutist switched from high to low octaves in an almost manic fashion, while the pianist pounded out a driving strain, the chaos transforming to a slow, mourning melodic line pouring out of the flute. Played in the lower octave, the sorrow permeated the minor tune. Returning to the original melody, the performers transposed the music into a minor key, showing the hero's acceptance but ending on a hollow chord, showing the waste of a human being.

The performers ended. Silence reigned. The audience paused and then resounded with applause. The final examination was over. Both students and performers acknowledged and understood the impact that innocence and corruption make.

Lauren and Courtney were not the only students to express their knowledge of romance and tragedy through music. Several students wrote original lyrics and music that they performed on guitar or piano, all of them portraying the optimism of man's original state, in which he has no limits and is in tune with the natural world, where he finds an escape from this life. However, each song ultimately became distorted as the piece transitioned to tragedy. Some of the students portrayed this movement with discordant sounds; one even scratched a turntable to create the confusion he wanted. Eventually, the protagonist realizes that he has wasted his life and suffers consequences because of his choices. One young man ended his guitar piece by quoting e. e. cummings's poem, "this is the passing of all shining things." Another student made a narrated tape of her playing the piano, with each stage of romance and tragedy depicted by a work of a well-known composer such as Mozart or Bach.

Some of the other assessment possibilities included writing a conversation that could occur among groupings of characters on the nature of romance or tragedy. The conversation could be a dialogue, an interview, or a panel discussion. Examples of the groupings included the two protagonists Othello and Gatsby and villains such as Shakespeare's Iago, Hawthorne's Chillingworth or Professor Baglioni, and Fitzgerald's Tom Buchanan. Two other trios of characters included victims—Hawthorne's Hester and Beatrice and Shakespeare's Desdemona—and troubled protagonists—Hawthorne's Dimmesdale, Paul from "Paul's Case," and Shane. Several students chose this option, coproducing a videotaped show in which the villains discussed their lack of conscience and their delight in seeing evil succeed. Also using video as their medium, several students wrote scripts depicting the tragic or romantic hero, the innocent victim, or people in search of a material paradise. Complete with costuming, props, camera angles, and memorized lines, their productions usually lasted 8 to 10 minutes.

I graded the pieces on the depth of thought (content) of the work, the creativity and imagination that they displayed, the amount of time and effort required to produce the final piece, and the overall effectiveness of the work. In addition to assigning the product, I required students to write analyses of what they attempted to do, with textual evidence or specific descriptions of how their pieces were to be interpreted. Most of these word-processed analyses were two to three pages long. Then, on the final examination day, students presented abstracts of their products to the class in a four- to five-minute explanation that either confirmed or altered the grade I had already assigned. I change very few grades.

Most students chose to write an original narrative poem, a children's story, or a short story. Many illustrated their work as well. One student chose to write the story "Finnigan's Fall" with Finnigan as a classic tragic hero. The author established the protagonist as a fish of high esteem possessing many natural abilities and talents, capable of many good deeds, and respected and admired by his peers. His greatest strength, as well as his greatest weakness, is his love of life's beauty. This flaw ultimately leads Finnigan down a tragic path.

Finnigan makes a disastrous choice to capture a moonbeam for himself, fulfilling a selfish pleasure and removing it from nature. Finnigan is myopic, seeing only the beauty and brilliance of the moonbeam, not stopping to realize that the object of his desire is not meant for him. This is the first step toward his fall. Thus, he makes himself vulnerable and accidentally jumps for a hook, mistaking it for a moonbeam, and suffers physical pain. Enlightened by his error, he realizes he has crossed a boundary and violated a code of nature. He realizes he must be punished and accepts his fate. Only after feeling remorse does he find redemption. Eventually, the fish of Aquatica, the region where he lives, memorialize him each time the moon shines down upon the ocean.

Some students chose to write poetry to illustrate the romance and tragedy story. In "Ashes, Ashes, We All Fall Down," the writer composed a narrative poem about a tree that symbolizes knowledge, strength, age, and character but that does not understand the importance of his position. Although he provides shelter and is regarded as heroic by the other creatures in the forest, he is dissatisfied, desiring whimsy and demonstrating man's inability to be in harmony with nature and himself. Instead, the tree wants to be as free as the wind. In the end, the tree realizes his value too late as he becomes the next victim of loggers. The writer made the point that the tree forgets his own identify and worth and finds it only in the process of dying.

A few students capitalized on their artistic talent. One young woman sculpted a pot with decorations illustrating three different types of tragedy: the flawed hero, the sacrificial hero, and the innocent victim. The vines on the outside of the pot symbolized the path of the heroine's life, illustrated by a ladybug. Beginning at an exalted stage, the protagonist is highly esteemed and regarded because she has accomplished a goal. As she continues on her path, she encounters a problem, a fork in the road. Either she can follow a widely curving path and reach her destination safely, or she can choose a straight path that plummets her into destruction. The artist represented the heroine's choices by vines that intersect the pot. When the ladybug errs, she falls to the underside of the pot and into chaos and suffering; she is redeemed only after acknowledging her mistake. Still, she must suffer the consequences of her actions, and to symbolize this, the sculptor relegated her final resting place to the bottom of the pot.

To illustrate the theme of the sacrificial hero, the artist carved the hands of Christ and the nails that pierced them at the base of the pot, supporting the rest of the structure as an indication of His willingness to die to save the human race.

For her final tragedy pattern, that of the innocent victim, the sculptor positioned a tulip in the center of the pot that must suffer because someone else has sinned. Removing the flower from its normal environment, the artist placed it in this terra cotta pot, an unnatural place. Through no fault of its own, the tulip is being strangled by the vines that surround it. The vines represent a distortion of nature and connect the tragic elements.

The students responded enthusiastically to this performance assessment strategy, expressing satisfaction with the tangible evidence of what they had learned. Agreeing that their preparation was more intense than studying for a paper-and-pencil exam, they overwhelmingly preferred the approach. Using their imagination and creativity stimulated them and rewarded them. Moreover, they truly shared in one another's endeavors, a sharp contrast to the isolated test or essay-writing experience. Both students and teacher came away from the experience assured that mastery learning had occurred.

Helpful Tips

1. Give the students sufficient time to prepare a worthwhile project.

2. Discuss the possibilities of each option in detail. Use models, if available.

3. Set the level of expectation so that the students understand the depth and challenge of the assignment.

4. Carefully outline what elements the analysis must contain.

▧ Language Arts

Debra Calvert
Waldorf, Maryland

I teach eighth-grade language arts/reading at John Hanson Middle School, a suburban school outside Washington, D.C. Our population consists of 898 students in grades 6, 7, and 8. The daily schedule includes eight instructional classes plus three lunch shifts. Each class is 42 minutes in length with 3 to 4 minutes built in for passing time in the hallways. Our school believes in the middle school philosophy that students should be introduced to a variety of experiences to explore their interests and talents. Therefore, we offer our eighth graders a variety of electives including band, chorus, technical education, home economics, physical education, and math applications.

Even though our students have the opportunity to explore a variety of related arts, core academics are the major focus. All students receive instruction in math, language arts/reading, science, and social studies. Our school system is unique in that students at the middle school level are enrolled in a double period of language arts/reading on a daily basis. This means that students receive a total of 84 minutes of instruction each day in the integrated content areas of reading, writing, and language usage. The only exception to this schedule is a small group of eighth graders (approximately 20%) that is enrolled in a single period of language arts/reading and a single period of foreign language—French or Spanish. These students are enrolled in our most rigorous academic courses, and their classes are designated as the top enrichment classes of our school. I have the challenge of teaching three classes made up of this unique population.

These classes are required to meet the same state and county outcomes as their peers in the regular double block, but they must do so with only half as much instructional time. To help students successfully meet the state and county requirements, I created a reading activity to help reinforce the reading and writing skills that are introduced in my instruction. What I call a "Reading Log" serves multiple purposes, but its primary goal is to ensure that the top enrichment students are reading for various purposes outside the regular school day and interacting with the text in a meaningful way.

In conjunction with our state assessments, the Maryland School Performance Assessment Program (MSPAP), and our local curriculum (Charles County, MD), reading is categorized into three purposes:

(a) reading to be informed, (b) reading for literary experience, and (c) reading to perform a task. The purposes for reading set the framework for the Reading Log activity. In this yearlong assignment, students are required to read for approximately 15 minutes for a minimum of three times during a two-week period. After reading, they follow a set of guidelines to help them think about the reading and to write their log entries. In my classes, students are required to complete and turn in three entries every two weeks. This time frame can be varied, but it enables me to thoughtfully grade each child's log and return it in a timely fashion.

The first step in completing each individual entry is to write a bibliographic citation for the reading. I require that students follow the Modern Language Association style format, as this is the format used by local high schools. Writing these citations helps students prepare for more complex tasks that they will encounter in high school when researching and writing papers.

Students practice writing citations for all types of sources, including books, magazine and journal articles, newspaper articles, anthologies, and Internet sites. After learning these techniques through this assignment, students are able to apply this knowledge, when applicable, in other content areas, such as writing a science fair report. Students also learn to read a works cited list in order to find references for information that they are researching. Working with sources helps students become more comfortable with compiling, reading, and using a works cited list in their future educational endeavors.

The second step in preparing to write the entry requires that the students read the material they have chosen and identify the reading purpose. To do this, students must analyze what they have read and categorize it as reading to be informed, reading for literary experience, or reading to perform a task. Identifying reading purposes is a daily part of our classroom instruction. Students learn to approach different texts using multiple strategies that enable them to become better, more active readers. By identifying the reading purpose for themselves, students can practice the skills and strategies taught in class and view a text from the perspective of a critical reader.

After reading and identifying the purpose, students then have the flexibility of self-selecting 1 of 10 topics to develop into a log entry (each of the purposes has its own set of 10 topics). The topics help students analyze the text from four stances:

1. Global understanding—The reader constructs meaning based on an overall understanding of the text.

2. Interpretation—The reader must revisit the text to clarify, verify, revise, and extend his or her global understandings.

3. Personal reflection and response—The reader uses prior knowledge and personal experience in interacting with the text in order to extend meaning.

4. Critical analysis—The reader must "step away" from the text and examine the author's perspective and craft.

These "stances" are included in the state outcomes and are the state's technique for measuring student comprehension in reading on the MSPAP. Through the use of the reading log, students are able to practice responding to stance activities and also receive feedback on their responses throughout the year. As a teacher, it is rewarding to see the improvement in the manner in which students respond to the activities.

Once a topic has been selected, students are required to develop that topic as completely as possible in paragraph form. Students must first address the topic by writing a clear opening statement for their entry. This helps the students focus their entry on one chosen idea. They must then provide examples or citations from the actual reading to support their topic sentence. For example, if a student chooses to write about the mood of a particular reading, he or she must provide clear examples or citations from the reading itself to prove that his or her analysis of mood is logical. Students are required to provide a minimum of three examples or citations from the reading in each entry. Students are also taught to extend on these examples to provide further explanation for the reader as to how or why the example supports the initial statement.

Each entry is carefully evaluated based on these elements. Being able to respond to a student's writing on a continual basis enables me as the teacher to give students more personalized feedback and help them improve various aspects of their written responses. I have noticed that student responses mature as the year progresses.

Student sentence structure and variety become more complex, and their word choice becomes more sophisticated. Their ability to cite information from a reading to support their ideas and opinions becomes more natural, and they begin to express logical connection to their audience. Students receive two grades on a biweekly basis, one for the collection of entries and one for their bibliographic citations. The suggestions and notes that I write for the students in their reading logs are reviewed by them and are used to improve their responses for the next turn-in date.

Although my initial goals for creating this reading log were to encourage reading outside the classroom, to promote reading for a variety of purposes, to help students analyze texts in a way other than summarizing, and to provide students with more practice in writing paragraphs that show support from texts, I found that another benefit was also present. I began to learn an incredible amount of information about my students by what they were reading and writing. This aspect of the reading log was totally unexpected, but it enabled me to establish a more personal rapport with each and every one of my students. Having a positive climate in the classroom is an essential component in successfully educating the youths of today. The reading log gave me another avenue through which to achieve this positive environment.

Since I began the assignment of reading logs three years ago, I have gained valuable insights about the children who are enrolled in my classroom. By learning about my students' interests, I am able to make a personal connection with students that I might not be able to achieve in the 42 minutes of class. Students read and write about a variety of topics that are of interest to them. Their topics range from the very serious, such as death, diseases, eating disorders, and divorce, to the less serious, including video games, sports, new hairstyles, music, and teen idols. Reading students' log entries has enabled me to see a side of them that I might otherwise not see in the classroom setting. Students write about their likes and dislikes, fears and worries, and interests and hobbies. Knowing more is an example of how this connection can take place, as the following example illustrates.

> Three years ago, I taught a class in which an extremely shy girl, Nicole, was enrolled. After speaking to the gifted and talented teacher, I learned that Nicole was placed into the top enrichment class after her sixth-grade year but that she lacked the self-esteem and confidence of her peers. The gifted and talented teacher also told me that Nicole was disappointed that she would have a different teacher for eighth-grade language arts/reading (this group had the same teacher for sixth and seventh grade). She had become comfortable with her former teacher and was hesitant to begin over again.
>
> As the year began, so did our reading log assignments. The weeks went by, and I noticed that Nicole was an excellent writer. I also noticed that all her log entries came from a magazine titled *Cats*. Her knowledge of cats was incredible, and her love for the animals was even more evident.
>
> About one month into the school year, my own cat ran away. While I was handing back reading logs in Nicole's class, I paused when I reached her desk. I quietly whispered to Nicole, "I wanted to tell you that my cat ran away—I knew you would understand"—. After class we talked, and she encouraged me that my cat would come home, based on what she knew about cat behavior. For two days Nicole came to me in the morning after she got off the bus asking if my cat had

returned. On the third day I was able to tell her that she had, and I could see the relief on Nicole's face. From that day on, Nicole and I had a special bond that transferred into the classroom.

Throughout my years of using the reading logs, I have discovered many benefits from using the activity. Its uses extend well beyond the academic purposes for which it was established. As a language arts teacher, I am always analyzing and evaluating students' writings, but this assignment creates a new twist by giving me the opportunity to learn about the student as a person first and a reader-writer second. Since its inception, I have modified the guidelines for the reading log each year and will continue to do so on an as-needed basis. One aspect that will remain the same, though, is my enthusiasm for learning about the feelings, emotions, interests, and attitudes of my students and for establishing a special rapport with each of them.

Helpful Tips

1. *Teach the guidelines.* I set aside at least one class period at the beginning of the school year to "walk through" the guidelines with the students. It is also a good "reading to perform a task" lesson, as is it organized by steps. I find that it is helpful to go through the entire process as a class, including the silent reading.

2. *Allow for multiple opportunities to practice citing sources.* Practice makes perfect, and this will be evident in future assignments.

3. *Read each entry very carefully.* Students will know immediately if the teacher is simply skimming their responses. Conversely, they will know when teachers have read in detail. Also, make personalized comments on the entries. Whether it is an answer to a question that the student has, a strategy to improve the paragraph, or a change in the way something is

worded, students can use these comments to improve on their future responses.

4. *Start small.* It may not be feasible for every teacher to do this type of activity with all classes or to collect every two weeks. Give yourself, as well as the students, enough time to complete the tasks.

5. *Use as an in-class activity.* With one of my lower-level classes, we participate in the reading log activity once a week during class time. Students complete one entry within that length of time. This structure makes the assignment easier for them to complete, and I have an opportunity to conference with each student on the progress of his or her reading and writing.

The Multicultural Independent Study

Terrie Saunders
Omaha, Nebraska

The sophomore honors English program at the school where I teach has a very traditional curriculum established by a curriculum committee. There is currently very little in the way of minority literature. However, one of the major attractions of the school where I teach is its diversity of cultures. Although the traditional curriculum may not allow for teaching much minority literature as a unit, it does allow for the use of minority literature in independent studies.

Students in my class must complete an independent reading project each semester. This independent reading is preapproved by me and by their parents. (I send home with each student a form that identifies the title of the selected book and requires a parent's signature.) The independent reading project requires students to read the book, write a paper, and give a speech. During the first semester, the focus is on nonfiction (specifically biography and autobiography); during the second semester, the focus is on the novel. Before handing out the materials, I discuss with students the importance of learning and understanding other cultures and viewpoints. I then tell the class that at least one of the two independent readings must be a work written by or about someone from a minority group.

For the first-semester choice, the biography or autobiography, I provide students with a list of minority figures from which they may choose. This list is a compilation of suggestions from staff members who have a background in minority literature (i.e., the instructors for African American History and Ethnic Studies, the librarian, etc.). I also take the suggestions from an organization of gifted minority students that I sponsor. I indicate that students are not required to select from my list—the list merely offers suggestions that they may use if they choose to do so.

As they first begin their independent reading, I provide students with a handout for the book analysis, which focuses on the subject's contribution or historical role. By giving students the topic for the book analysis when they first begin reading, I let them know what to look for as they read. After students have read the books and written their reports, they then present a brief synopsis of the book, commenting on the qualities that led to the person's success, the events that had an impact on his or her life, or how this person's life has affected society today. This provides a speech opportunity and provides encouragement for other students to read the same book for personal enjoyment.

By the second semester, students have had the opportunity to discuss novels in class. They are therefore prepared to use their analytical skills independently on their own selected novel. Building on the foundations for an in-depth study of a literary work, which students have had from middle school and from first-semester in-class readings, I review the basics of literary analysis. Depending on the ability level of the students, this might be in the form of a review of such basic elements as theme, style, character motivation, and so forth, or it might mean an introduction to formal literary criticism. Those students who did not select a minority piece for the first semester's independent reading must do so for this project. Once again, before handing out the materials, I discuss with students the importance of learning and understanding other cultures and viewpoints. I also ask students to return a form with a parent's signature giving approval for the selected book.

I provide students with two handouts. The first outlines for students the requirements of the analytical paper. (By this time, students have written numerous expository papers and have discussed in detail numerous literary works.) The second handout is a list of appropriate works from which students may choose. This list is a compilation of books on the approved reading list for my school district, as well as suggestions from staff members and students who have a background in minority literature.

As with the first-semester paper, students present their papers in the form of a speech. Students comment on some literary aspect of the novel, with the instruction that they are to provide enough information so that their audience can understand the content without giving away the conclusion of the novel.

Each semester I ask those students who have chosen a minority work to complete a book review form for minority literature. This document asks basic questions regarding stereotyping issues, common experiences, and appropriate language and situations. I keep these forms on file to document that each of my students has, in fact, selected a minority work at least once during the school year and also to assist students in book choices in future years. If students are especially enthusiastic about a particular work, I suggest that they submit the work to the school district's committee that approves supplementary works. This gives students an opportunity to understand the process of book selections and to have an impact on the possible choices.

With this unit, I hope that students become aware of both the stereotyping in their own contacts and the stereotyping that is part of the literature they read. Ideally, they will be able to compare and contrast the attitudes developed from their outside reading with the in-class reading assignments. Another goal is to expand students' cultural awareness. Reading about someone who is from a minority background may give some insight into the lives of other people they may encounter, if not in high school, then in college or in the workplace. Finally, I encourage students to read literature that is from outside their own culture with the idea that the attitudes, beliefs, hopes, and dreams of all people are basically the same.

Helpful Tips

1. I give students the informational handouts early in their reading process so that they know what to look for as they read.

2. I work closely with parents on this project, encouraging parents to help students make selections and to read the books along with their students. I also encourage parents to fill out the book review for minority literature and the form for the selection of supplemental works.

3. I require parents to sign a form indicating their approval of the selected book. This eliminates any "fallout" regarding students' reading books that parents may consider inappropriate.

Chinese Literature and Culture, Lesson 1

Wanda Jones Thomas
Tulsa, Oklahoma

As one unit in a senior English class of world literature, the Chinese contributions are introduced, along with a few works studied in more depth. However, these works set the stage for my students, none of whom have traveled in or near China. I wanted a unit that would enable students to immerse themselves in the culture of these Asian peoples. The study of these broad schools of thought is a framework for the fiction and nonfiction materials to follow. Once students have seen the culture as a blending of three belief or thought systems, the literature, art, architecture, and music take on a depth of meaning not possible from just reading short stories or poems as pieces of literature divorced from the milieu of the culture.

My rationale for this method of beginning is that the more students are involved in controlling their own education, the more they will demand quality if they see the need for the skill or the information. Also, students will practice working in teams, just as they will be expected to do in the business world. This lesson works for all learning styles as well. Students are welcome to bring to the presentation whatever skills or ideas they have as a way to communicate to their peers what they find in the research. Dramatic, artistic, musical, kinesthetic, and other modes or styles of learning are limited only by the imagination of the groups. Technology is available in the building in computers, scanners, color printers, televisions, VCRs, digital cameras, PowerPoint or other programs, and other personal equipment owned by students or other teachers.

A spirit of team teaching allows students to interview teachers in other departments for input. For example, one social studies teacher has volunteered to share materials for student use, including purchases of Chinese artifacts, for the presentations. An art teacher has agreed to work with students if they want to produce something in the art room. The library/media specialist is available to help students in production using technology.

Bulletin board displays give students a chance to shine if they want to prepare something special. These display items can be wise sayings or information to be added to the time line, and again, these are limited only by imagination. For example, a seamstress could prepare doll clothes to evoke dynasties. An artist could draw or paint dragons or other creatures or scenes to illuminate the geography or culture, along with the normal additions of dates and names.

Helpful Tips

Because one whole wall in my classroom is a bulletin board, the time line fits extremely well, as it stretches across 3,500 years. However, the same idea could be used on a smaller scale, because the purpose is to enable global learners to see the big picture and for others to place details in perspective as we move from dynasty to dynasty, rather than decade to decade as students are used to learning in U.S. history classes.

The first time I handed out the assignment sheet, I underestimated student involvement and did not provide enough time for them to plan. The second year, handouts were available two weeks before we actually began the unit. One group produced (either made, rented, or borrowed) authentic costumes to deepen the understanding and relevance of their presentation. The girls practiced the short steps and humble attitudes of Chinese women. The guys made long hairstyles and mustaches to add to their authentic appearance. The excellence of their 15-minute presentation made their peers sorry that the skit was not longer. As a result of that team's work, two students, at the urging of their teammates, asked the drama teacher if they could be included in the next school play.

A teacher never knows the impact of a lesson, a comment, or an opportunity until some result such as this comes about. Careful preparation, attention to details, a place for each student's ability and potential, and an atmosphere in the classroom of mutual respect—all of these work together to touch young lives in ways that will enable students to broaden their views of the world and their places within it.

State Standards

Many PASS objectives are fulfilled in this unit:

I. *Reading process.* A. Vocabulary. Knowledge of words and word meanings. Students are building a personal vocabulary through study of the three words and peripheral learning of words as they pre-pare to discuss and to interpret the particular "ism" for the class.

I. B. Comprehension. Ability to interact with words and con-cepts to understand what the writer has said. 4. Skim text for overall impression and scan text for particular information. They must de-cide which parts to use in discussing the meaning and in transferring that information to the task of the assignment, which is to illuminate the meaning of a Chinese poem by placing it in the context of the cul-tural way of thinking and the values inherent therein.

II. *Responding to text.* A. Recall and organize information, make inferences, and draw conclusions by using story structure.

II. D. Evaluate works of world literature as reflections of time and culture. In order to explain a short poem for the class, the group must first understand the school of thought out of which the poem arose and see it as a reflection of a particular way of thinking and liv-ing in China.

II. I. Use knowledge of literary genre and text structures to aid comprehension. Whether the group uses a poem or a short story, the basic structure must be part of the explanation.

II. K. Analyze details for relevancy and accuracy.

II. L. Discuss underlying theme or message when interpreting fiction and poetry.

II. M. Analyze the poet's use of imagery, personification, symbol-ism, and figures of speech. Of course, Chinese poetry may seem decep-tively simple until one learns to look through the eyes of Confucius, Buddha, or the Tao to find the meaning between the lines.

II. N. Explain how the use of sound devices in poetry supports the subject and mood (e.g., rhyme, rhythm, alliteration, and onomatopoeia).

III. *Information and research.* A. Use suitable research methods to elicit and present evidence from primary and secondary sources.

As the students search for material for their presentations, they must approach various sources and judge whether the information is suitable for their purposes.

III. E. Understand technical directions to complete tasks (e.g., home or auto repair, use of computer software, assembling equipment) as appropriate to content area curriculum. Various pieces of technology are available, but students are responsible for preparation and use of them.

III. J. Analyze, synthesize, evaluate, summarize, and paraphrase information from multiple sources. Because students will be limited to a 15-minute presentation, material must be succinct.

IV. *Effective reading habits.* D. Read for a variety of purposes such as for pleasure, to gain information, to communicate, or to support an opinion.

VII. *Listening and speaking.* A. Demonstrate thinking skills in listening, speaking, reading, and writing. For example, students, individually or in groups, will gather information, organize and analyze it, and generate a report that conveys ideas clearly and relates to the background and interest of the audience.

VII. B. Prepare, organize, and deliver oral responses to literary works.

VII. I. Distinguish between speaker's opinion and verifiable facts.

VII. K. 2. Speak responsibly to present accurate, truthful, and ethical messages.

VIII. *Visual literacy.* E. Access information from a variety of media (television, computers, videos, CD-ROMs) and evaluate the quality of material selected.

IX. *Literature.* D. Read and respond to historically or culturally significant works of literature. For example, students are expected to find ways to clarify the ideas and make connections between literary works.

UNIT: Chinese Literature and Culture

TEXTBOOKS

Blunden, C., & Elvin, M. (1998). *Cultural atlas of China* (Rev. ed., G. Speake, Ed.). Abingdon, UK: Andromeda Oxford Limited.

Ebrey, P. B. (Ed.). (1993). *Chinese civilization: A sourcebook* (2nd ed.). New York: Free Press.

Murphey, R. (1997). *East Asia: A new history.* New York: Longman.

The literature of China. (1993). In *World literature.* Austin, TX: Holt, Rinehart & Winston.

BULLETIN BOARD

Quote (from pp. 510-511 in Holt, Rinehart and Winston book):

To the Chinese, poetry has always been an exercise for the mind and the spirit rather than a purely literary pursuit. In keeping with Confucian, Taoist, and Buddhist thought, Chinese poetry often involves the contemplation of nature and the search for harmony between the inner and outer worlds. Chinese poetry is almost exclusively lyrical. Its essence is the exploration of passing feelings and impressions.

LESSON PLAN 1

Objective: To evaluate the contributions of Confucianism, Taoism, and Buddhism to Chinese literature.

Assignment 1

Choose one of the three systems of thought and register your choice with me. Come to class prepared for group work (three, four, or five students) to determine your group's presentation of your choice.

Assignment 2

Prepare an annotated bibliography of the sources you actually use for the presentation. Each person in the group must have his or her own bibliography page. See the sample on the south bulletin board.

Assignment 3

Each group will choose one method of presentation:

1. Panel discussion

2. Speeches with each member participating

3. PowerPoint (Make arrangements to have the media hookup for the computer.)

4. Original words, music, or both, with or without a skit

5. Other (If you have a better idea, let's talk about it.)

(If you are absent on the day your group presents, you will make your own presentation the next day you return to class. Be prepared to do so without pleading ignorance of this work, and be sure you have your own visuals, poem, and notes that day.)

Assignment 4

Presentations will be given during class (15 minutes for each group). Consider these aspects:

1. Definition of your choice (the "ism")

2. Visuals (poster, painting, pictures, artifacts, handouts, etc.)

3. Information to add to the time line on the west bulletin board

4. Poem (Be prepared to explain it in terms of your "ism.")

Assignment 5

Bonus: The time line will be established on the west bulletin board. Anyone who volunteers to come in before or after school or during the lunch period to help will receive bonus points for the work. See me if you are interested so that we can discuss the process involved and hear suggestions on how to carry out this project.

▨ Succeeding With Reading and Writing Instructions and Learning Tolerance by Studying Another Culture Through Literature: Chinese Literature and Culture, Lesson 2

Wanda Jones Thomas
Tulsa, Oklahoma

As a follow-up lesson to the study of Confucianism, Buddhism, and Taoism and their contributions to Chinese literature and culture (Lesson 1), this unit of fiction and nonfiction selections from various books enables students to build upon the foundation of understanding and to move further into seeing the Chinese people as humans just like themselves in many ways.

The textbooks listed on the handout are just a few of the many books now available about China, all having been published in the past decade. Excellent commentary enriches these stories and encourages thoughtful discussion and insight into the minds of a people who are very mysterious because they are a world away from our homes. Students especially enjoy finding quotable quotes to display on the bulletin board. Looking for these quotes is an excellent method of working toward theme in literature. A book with no succinct thoughts leaves the mind hungry for something worthwhile, something more than the cotton candy offered by many of the books students choose to read. By calling attention to this strength of good literature, I hope to raise my students' expectations of the books they read for pleasure.

My rationale for this lesson is that the more we understand other people, the better chance we have of peaceful world relations and, just as important, the more we understand ourselves as citizens in a shrinking world. Tolerance must begin somewhere, and a good story is an enjoyable place to begin. A small percentage of students in our Tulsa schools are from other countries, but these students are valuable as resources because they can give firsthand accounts of experiences in their culture, either their own or a family member's.

One student who wrote in a Chinese dialect fascinated the class by showing some classmates how to write their names in Chinese. A valued artifact from China, personal stories, perhaps even a demonstration of the Chinese language by a native speaker—these are more valuable than we know because we cannot guess the far-reaching effects of having a face and a name instead of merely a concept of hundreds of millions of people living somewhere a long way off.

This unit usually takes 5 to 10 school days, depending on the ability level of the class and how long it takes them to read the material. Some reading is done at home, but some is done in class so that students can hear stories read aloud and so that comments can be made within the stories as well as in the class discussion at the end.

Helpful Tips

One must be sensitive to students' belief systems and family traditions. Although classes have been mixed with a few students from other countries, the majority of my students are white, black, and Native American. A few students from diverse backgrounds, including Vietnam, Laos, Germany, China, Japan, and India, prove my theory of the need for global understanding. The input of their racial, ethnic, and religious traditions has enriched this unit beyond what I expected.

The first time I taught this unit, I began with a journal entry titled "Who Are You and Why Are You Here?" I admit my expectations were for most of the students to say that they were seniors and that they had to have senior English to graduate, period, end of entry. I stand amazed sometimes by the depth of thought that is engendered in students by so simple an assignment. Some of the responses made me laugh; some made me shed a few tears. All responses made me a better teacher as I raised my expectations to meet the challenges of why the students were in my class. Because this senior class is the last chance that students will have to learn communication skills before they face the responsibilities of adulthood, I feel a lot of frustration because I want them to learn everything I can squeeze into our class. Nevertheless, I believe a few lessons learned well are better than all lessons merely skimmed. This unit gives the students a cursory overview of a people who deserve our admiration and our thanks for the many aspects of civilization they have shared with the world. I would like to teach a whole semester of Asian literature, but time does not afford that privilege in a world literature course in high school. Nevertheless, perhaps I have opened eyes to other worlds, suggested that learning about other people can be edifying, or started thought processes in directions that will touch tomorrow and make the future better for someone.

The last Assignment is a 5- to 7-paragraph essay; students can focus on either of the texts from assignments 3 through 7, they may use two or more texts for a comparison paper, or they may compare one or more to life in the United States. Five school days are given for this homework assignment—to write, to polish, and to hand in their essays. After papers have been handed in, students have the opportunity to read their essays to the class. A few volunteer to read theirs aloud, and a few others invite friends to read theirs.

With student's permission, I make overhead transparencies of especially good parts of the essays. An especially well-written introductory or concluding paragraph deserves to be seen and heard and is an excellent teaching tool to show students what can be done. Peer evaluation and applause serve two goals: The writer is vindicated for the hard work he or she has done, and struggling students see their classmates achieving and get valuable tips on producing these paragraphs. Middle paragraphs also are used to show various methods of adding commentary, inserting quoted material, and concluding a middle paragraph with a closing sentence.

This part of the lesson gave one student the courage to admit he is writing a book. He had not shared this information with me, but the applause of classmates for his outstanding writing gave him the opportunity to announce the fact to the class. He was congratulated and encouraged by the response of his peers. What a wonderful outcome for him. He has promised to send me a first copy signed when he publishes. It could happen. He already has a fan club.

State Standards

Many of the standards of PASS are fulfilled in this unit:

I. *Reading process.* A. Vocabulary. 1. Continue to build personal vocabulary through word study, the reading of literature, and class discussion (e.g., multiple meanings, dictionary definitions, and meanings in context). 6. Understand and explain shades of meaning in related words (e.g., *softly* and *quietly*). B. Comprehension. Read and comprehend both fiction and nonfiction that is appropriately designed for grade-level reading. 7. Vary reading speed and strategies according to the type of material and the purpose for reading. C. Fluency. 2. Continue to read with expression, interjecting a sense of feeling, anticipation, or characterization.

II. *Responding to text.* H. Use text organization as an aid to comprehension of increasingly difficult content material (e.g., compare-contrast, cause-effect, problem-solution, sequential order). 3. Summarize fiction and nonfiction by determining the main idea and supporting details.

IV. *Effective reading habits.* C. Respond to oral reading led by teacher through discussion, art, drama, and writing.

IV. B. Read, discuss, and analyze short stories, novels, essays, speeches, technical documents, and other works representing diversity (e.g., gender, ethnicity, and nationality).

V. *Writing.* A. Use a writing process to develop and refine composition skills. B. Write a variety of narrative, descriptive, expository, persuasive, and reflective compositions that establish and support a central idea with a thesis statement; supporting paragraphs with facts, details, explanations, or examples; and a concluding paragraph that summarizes the points.

VI. *Grammar/usage and mechanics.* A. Demonstrate appropriate practices in speaking and writing. Students are expected to write using complete sentences and edit for usage, mechanics, and spelling.

VI. B. Demonstrate correct use of standard English.

IX. *Literature.* A. Demonstrate a knowledge of and an appreciation for various forms of literature.

UNIT: Chinese Literature and Culture

TEXTBOOKS

Blunden, C., & Elvin, M. (1998). *Cultural atlas of China* (Rev. ed., G. Speake, Ed.). Abingdon, UK: Andromeda Oxford Limited.

Ebrey, P. B. (Ed.). (1993). *Chinese civilization: A sourcebook* (2nd ed.). New York: Free Press.

Murphey, R. (1997). *East Asia: A new history.* New York: Longman.

The literature of China. (1993). In *World literature.* Austin, TX: Holt, Rinehart & Winston.

Chinese literature 1000 B.C.-A.D. 1890. (1991). In E. Thompson et al. (Eds.), *World literature.* Englewood Cliffs, NJ: Prentice Hall.

DOCUMENTARY FILMS

Gibney, F. (Executive Director). (1992). *The Pacific century* [10-part videocassette series]. Seattle, WA: Pacific Basin Institute with KCTS/Seattle. (60 minutes each: 10 hours.)

BULLETIN BOARD

Quote: Receive bonus points for finding a worthwhile quote.

Quote: (from p. 260 in Ebrey, 1993)

To listen to others and not to examine your own mind is to be manipulated by circumstances.

LESSON PLAN 2

Objective: To understand Chinese culture through literature.

Assignment 1
See the language explanations on p. xv in Murphey (1997). Practice the sounds of Chinese. See "Language, Writing and Calligraphy" (pp. 178-183) in Blunden and Elvin (1998).

Assignment 2
See the time chart on pp. xix-xx in Murphey (1997). See the chronological table (pp. 8-9) in Blunden and Elvin (1998). Add pertinent information to the time line on the west bulletin board.

Assignment 3
Read "The Metal Bound Box" (pp. 6-7) from the Classical Period in Ebrey (1993). Discuss the religious beliefs and governmental requirements referenced in the story.

Assignment 4
Read "Human Nature Is Bad" (pp. 25-26) in Murphey (1997). Discuss the conclusions reached by Confucius regarding Mencius's statement.

Assignment 5
Read "The Missing Axe" (p. 549) in the Holt, Rinehart and Winston book. Discuss the Taoist "point" hidden here.

Assignment 6
Read "The Dancing Horses of Xuanzong's Court" (pp. 123-124) in Ebrey (1993). Discuss the attitude toward foreign influences ca. A.D. 740.

Assignment 7

Read "Wherein Lies the Way Out for Me?" by Li Jing (pp. 484-487) in Ebrey (1993). Compare the plight of this young, college-educated wife and mother with her counterpart in the United States.

Assignment 8

Write a 5- to 7-page essay to conclude this study of the different aspects of Chinese culture. Either choose one of the texts, compare two or more, or compare to life in the United States. *Due 6 school days from today.*

CHAPTER **3**

Succeeding With Mathematics Instruction

T his is the place to read how your colleagues are succeeding with mathematics instruction.

 **Chapter Overview**

■ **Linda E. Hains**, a math/science program coordinator at Rock Hill High School in Rock Hill, South Carolina, uses real-life applications for the mathematical concepts of data collection, graphical representation, statistical analysis, and prediction.

■ **Jenny W. Holmstrom,** a national board certified math teacher at Sumner High School in Sumner, Washington, designed this lesson for use in her Calculus class, but it can also be used in Precalculus and Advanced Algebra.

■ **Jenny W. Holmstrom,** a national board certified math teacher at Sumner High School in Sumner, Washington, says "the purpose for using instructional videotapes is twofold, to provide an alternative to lecture and note taking and to incorporate applications outside of a classroom setting."

■ **Eileen Stewart,** a teacher at Cypress Creek High School in Orlando, Florida, believes "factoring is so necessary to the students' success in mathematics. I give it special emphasis."

■ **Linda E. Hains,** a math/science program coordinator at Rock Hill High School in Rock Hill, South Carolina, has her students collect the daily population figures for the world and for the United States for one month

▨ What's Your Sport?
A Statistical Challenge

Linda E. Hains
Rock Hill, South Carolina

GRADES
   10 to 12

SUBJECTS
   Mathematics, physical education, statistics, technology

OVERVIEW
   In this project, students will use real-life applications of the mathematical concepts of data collection, graphical representation,

statistical analysis, and prediction using a TI-82 graphing calculator, the Internet, and Microsoft's *Encarta CD-ROM Encyclopedia.*

Students will be directed to the ESPN Sportszone on the Internet. They will select a sport of their choice to analyze using one- and two-variable statistical analysis. Microsoft's *Encarta* will also be used as a research tool for data collection.

Students will create histograms, scatterplots, and box and whisker plots to make predictions and comparisons based on the data they collect.

OBJECTIVES

In this activity, students will:

1. Research a sport of their choice using the ESPN Sportszone Internet site or Microsoft *Encarta*

2. Collect data on their sport and determine one-variable statistical analysis on their data by creating histograms and box and whisker plots

3. Determine the highest 25% median, 75% lowest data point, and frequency of their data

4. Determine bivariable statistical analysis by creating and interpreting scatterplots

5. Calculate prediction equations and regression equations based on their data

6. Make predictions using a "line of best fit" equation

MATERIALS

This activity requires the following resources:

■ Internet ESPN Sportszone (http://espnet.sportszone.com/)

■ Microsoft *Encarta*

- TI-82 graphing calculator

- TI GraphLink

- Microsoft Works or Word and Excel (optional—for writing up oral reports)

PROCEDURE

The students will be divided into groups of three to four students. They will use the Internet or Microsoft Encarta to research and collect data about a sport of their choice. They may choose football, tennis, auto racing, or others.

After students collect statistics from their favorite sport, they must determine what type of graph would best represent their data. Using GraphLink, students will capture their statistical graphs and create documents using Microsoft Works. Students will perform analysis on their data and make predictions based on their findings. To conclude, the students will give oral presentations showing what predictions could be made based on their data and will provide extension questions for others to answer using the graphs and data.

Questions students are required to answer for this exercise include the following:

- Why did you choose to represent your data in the types of graphs you chose?

- Do the data points seem to fit in a straight line or a curve?

- What are some of the factors that would contribute to these results?

- What would be a line of best fit for your data?

- How did you determine your line of best fit?

- Do your data appear to have a perfect association, positive association, or no association?

■ What predictions can you make from your data?

BACKGROUND

To provide my students with the necessary skills to perform the statistical analysis, we studied how to enter data into a graphing calculator and how to determine the mean, median, and mode. We also created histograms, box and whisker graphs, and scatterplots. As we were working with the various types of graphs, we discussed when and how to use the graphs.

To prepare my students for the technological skills that were required for this project, we studied the population of the United States on the Internet. We also practiced capturing the screen of a graphing calculator and creating documents using Microsoft Works. (Microsoft Word or Excel could also be used.) Many of the students had weak graphing and computer skills before the project, but all of them acquired many new technology skills by the end.

By encouraging my students to find data that were meaningful and current through the Internet and *Encarta,* I was able to make statistical analysis more interesting. Our unit on linear functions became a real-life experience instead of just another math concept in the textbook.

RESOURCES

The primary resources for this project are as follows:

Microsoft *Encarta*

Texas Instruments graphing calculator

Internet: ESPN Sportszone

For articles, maps, or other media pertaining to this topic, look up the following in *Encarta Encyclopedia*:

Automobile racing

Baseball

Basketball

Boxing

Football

Golf

Hockey

Rugby football

Soccer

Tennis

Professional sports

Statistics

For additional online information and media, view the following *Encarta* articles:

Professional sports

Statistics

For additional relevant information, visit the following Web sites:

1. NASCAR Online (http://www.nascar.com/): NASCAR Online provides information about the stock-car circuit, including news, driver biographies and interviews, statistics, and schedules.

2. Total Baseball (http://www.totalbaseball.com/): Total Baseball is an online encyclopedia of baseball, with biographies of notable players, team histories, and the complete statistics for every player who has ever put on a professional uniform.

3. NBA.com (http://www.nba.com): The official site of the National Basketball Association includes news, interviews, features, standings, statistics, and numerous images.

4. International Boxing Hall of Fame (http://www.ibhof.com): The home page of the International Boxing Hall of Fame provides historical information about professional and amateur boxing, current boxing news and schedules, and biographies of inductees.

5. National Football League (http://www.nando.net/SportServer/football/nfl.html)

6. PGA Tour.com (http://pgatour.com): The official home page of the Professional Golfers' Association contains news and information about the organization and its tournaments.

7. Major League Soccer (http://www.mlsnet.com): The official home page of Major League Soccer provides news, results, feature articles, a guide to the teams, and other resources.

Helpful Tips

- Explain how to develop a good hypothesis and what type of research is required to prove or disprove a hypothesis.

- Be prepared to use time outside class for the students to conduct their research. (I opened the computer lab before school, during lunch, and after school several times a week while the students were gathering data.)

- Don't let students to change their hypothesis to fit their data. (It is just as correct to mathematically disprove your hypothesis as to prove the hypothesis.)

- Develop a weighted rubric to grade the presentations.

Using Boxes, Philosophy, and Art to Explain Limits

Jenny W. Holmstrom
Sumner, Washington

The State of Washington has enacted a new statewide test called the Washington Assessment of Student Learning (WASL) that all students must pass beginning in the year 2004 in order to graduate from a Washington State high school. The math concepts on the WASL have a strong communications component. It is not enough for students to be able to solve a mathematical problem—they must also explain in writing how they solved the problem. Their responses are scored on a rubric. Math teachers throughout the state have been focusing on improving the communications aspect in all mathematics courses so students will have experience writing about mathematics at all content levels.

This lesson is one I designed for use in my Calculus class, but it can be used in Precalculus as well, and pieces can be lifted and altered for inclusion in concepts taught in Advanced Algebra. I originally designed this series of activities to allow my Calculus students to understand the concept of limits in an applications sense: visually, graphically, and theoretically.

I begin the activity by giving each student a sheet of graph paper and having each student cut a square out of each corner. Each student is given a different side length for his or her square, beginning with a one-by-one square and increasing one unit for each student in the class. The students are directed to fold the remaining part of the sheet of graph paper into an open-faced box. When this is done, all the boxes are laid out for the class to examine, and the students are asked to guess which box will hold the largest volume.

I draw a chart on the board that matches the chart on their worksheets and have each student come up and write his or her box's dimensions and volume in the appropriate row. I ask the class to examine the chart for patterns and then to identify the box with the largest volume. Some are surprised at the results.

I give the students time to answer the questions on the Box Problem worksheet, and then we discuss them as a class. I spend time explaining how to build the formula for the volume of the box based on the size of the graph paper we used. I display the graph on an overhead graphing calculator and take time to have the class analyze the different features of the graph. I do this to make sure there are no misconceptions and to make sure all the students can correctly graph and change the window coordinates to show a good representation of the problem. I also take time to make clear to the students which parts of the cubic graph are not relevant to the problem.

I explain to the class how this problem relates to limits at a value, telling them that in the box problem there is a maximum volume that can be made out of the piece of graph paper they were given. Exact dimensions can be calculated using a cubic formula and the calculator.

Next, I read the class a short play from the book *Gödel, Escher, Bach* by Douglas Hofstadter. The play is a dialogue between the characters Achilles and a tortoise. They are discussing Zeno's Paradox as it relates to their famous footrace. The students enjoy the short play, and it adds an interesting dimension to the math class.

After reading about Zeno's Paradox, I give each student another piece of graph paper and direct the class to cut their pieces of paper into large squares (usually 50 by 50). I give the class colored pencils and ask them to divide their squares in half and color only half of their squares. I then direct them to divide the remaining half in half again and to color just half of that. I ask them to keep repeating the process until they can go no further. It does not matter if students divide the square in half diagonally, vertically, or horizontally, but some choices give more interesting patterns than others do. It is fun when students choose different methods, and they can all be viewed at the end of the activity.

I give the students time to answer the questions on the Zeno's Paradox worksheets. When they have answered everything they can, I ask them to explain the connection to the play I read them and the drawing activity. I ask them to explain the connection between limits and the drawing.

I explain how the equation $y = 1/2^x$ is derived, and we analyze its graph on the overhead graphing calculator. I again lead the students in a discussion of which parts of the graph are not relevant to the actual problem.

I have found that through exposure to this series of activities, the class's understanding of limits and their uses becomes very clear. This is also a very good activity for teaching that graphs are models for real situations and that often the entire graph is not used in actuality, so students become more aware of the fact that only pieces of the graph relate to a given problem.

This series of activities usually takes two 90-minute class periods to complete. Sumner High School operates on a four-period day block schedule. Students take four 90-minute classes each day, and classes are one semester long. The lesson can be broken into smaller parts and conducted over a longer period of time.

Helpful Tips

1. Using graph paper with large squares makes it easier to cut the squares out of the corners. With a large class of students, two can cut the same-size square.

2. Make a chart on butcher paper to tape to the wall or use a flip chart for students to record their results.

3. Each student should use at least two different colors for the coloring activity. Neat patterns emerge this way.

4. The book *Gödel, Escher, Bach* can be ordered from a local bookstore. It adds a nice philosophical connection to the idea of limits.

Integrating Instructional Video in the Classroom

Jenny W. Holmstrom
Sumner, Washington

I was part of a project called Mathline a few years ago that involved working with a local television station, KCTS channel 9 in Seattle, Washington. Included in the project were different strategies for using instructional videos in the classroom. Participants received training on techniques such as playing a video without the sound so students can identify characteristics from a film, incorporating closed captioning for use with English as a second language students, and using small increments of a video at a time. I designed an introductory statistics lesson modeling some of these techniques.

For the introductory statistics lesson, I chose to use portions of two videotapes. The first was titled "Shooting Stats" from an ESPN2 segment about sports figures. The second, *For All Practical Purposes,* came from the Annenberg/Center for Public Broadcasting Collection, and I used Program 6-7, which is a statistics overview.

The purpose for using instructional videotapes is twofold: to provide an alternative to lecture and note taking and to incorporate applications outside the classroom setting. Instead of watching entire videotapes, of which all minutes are not necessarily important, it is advantageous to choose certain parts of the video and view only those parts. In this way, the teacher can structure the lesson around certain concepts and integrate practice and review throughout the lesson.

I chose portions of the Annenberg video that described and defined definitions of key statistical terms such as *bias, sample, random, raw data, mean,* and *median.* Instead of just hearing the definitions, students were able to hear someone else describe the terms and give examples ranging from baseball to the U.S. census. Prior to watching the video, students were given a list of words to define. As the video segment began, a student was in charge of pausing the tape when a key word was defined. This enabled students time to record notes as they viewed, which kept them actively involved in the information.

After key words were introduced and explained, I would pause the video and have students practice finding some of the new terms. For example, a segment showed how census workers went from house to house to gather information on average incomes. I would stop the tape and ask students to give the amount of money they had earned from work the previous week. These amounts were recorded on the board, and as a class we used the data to calculate the mean. We then discussed whether our sample could be generalized to all students or whether our answer was biased in any way.

The next segment we viewed described and discussed the median. I paused the video and had the students calculate the median of their wages. By incorporating the videotapes in this manner, there was a reason for the students to pay attention. We practiced and reviewed as we went along, and everyone was actively engaged in the lesson.

There is a wealth of video material made for instructional purposes. Often, teachers must decide whether the whole video is worth watching or not use it at all. These techniques provide yet another alternative—choosing just a portion of a tape and using it for a very specific purpose. In this way, teachers are able to make better use of the class time they have available. These techniques can be used in any subject area.

Helpful Tips

1. Always view the tape in advance. Use a display counter to mark the beginnings of any segments you wish to use in class

so you do not have to waste time trying to fast-forward to a particular segment in the middle of class.

2. Create worksheets as you preview the video. You can tailor the worksheets to stress key points you want students to learn and understand.

3. Pause often during viewing to check for understanding and to get feedback.

4. Incorporate class activities into the viewing session that enable the students to practice material related to the tape and also related to their interests.

5. Don't be afraid to use more than one video and to watch only a few minutes of each. Not all videos show material you want students exposed to at one time. It is OK to pick and choose and to design your own lesson. No two teachers teach the same material in the same manner and with the same focus.

6. If the beginning of a video is important for understanding the context of an example but you don't have time to show the whole tape, summarize the first segment for the class so they understand the context of the segment they are about to view.

Extensions

The following are some Web sites to investigate and use in classroom activities involving statistics:

■ Links to statistical materials:
http://www.dartmouth.edu/~chance/

■ Links to math subjects:
http:/www.forum.swathmore.edu/index. survey98/html

▧ Factoring Fiesta

Eileen Stewart
Orlando, Florida

Factoring polynomials has been a hot topic in our math teachers' lounge lately. The reason? The Algebra II classes are in the midst of factoring, and the Algebra I teachers are looking for any piece of information that may help them next month when their classes will be factoring. The main area of discussion is factorable trinomials. An interesting sideline to these discussions is that the teachers of advanced classes think trial and error is the best method. The teachers of regular classes know that their students do best when they have procedures to follow that will always lead to the correct answers. Talk to the other teachers at your school and find a new way to teach a lesson.

Factoring is used throughout the algebra curriculum: when working with polynomial expressions, solving quadratic equations and inequalities, and graphing parabolas. The connection between the solutions of a quadratic equation and its graph is an essential part of Algebra II. Factoring is also used in later courses. The students need factoring skills to prove trigonometric identities and to solve trigonometric equations.

Because factoring is so necessary to the students' success in mathematics, I give it a special emphasis. I host a Factoring Fiesta the evening before the last factoring test in Algebra II. Students and parents are invited to a 90-minute practice session. I vary the time but usually start at 6:30 p.m.

The class rules are relaxed for the night. Students are encouraged to interrupt with "I'm lost," which results in an explanation. Students may work at any desk, the board, and the overhead. I encourage them to steer the direction of the content. They tell me in which area they need help, and we do several problems in that area until they feel confident. The students help each other and may talk in small groups while I am working with the rest of the students. This is a chance for any student to review any part of the factoring lessons again.

The students think the best part of the night is the food. I make brownies and chili cheese dip with tortilla chips. The students bring in other treats as well. Many of the students prepare a special dish themselves. There is usually one dish the students really enjoy. Whoever brought that dish gets quite a bit of attention, which the "chef" loves. The students have a plate full of food while working, which is a treat in my no-eating-in-class room.

Because my school is on the four-by-four schedule, my class time is precious. This fiesta is a relaxed atmosphere, and there is no bell, so if we need more time, we stay. It provides a chance for the students to individually have my full attention for as long as they need it.

About half the class usually attends the Factoring Fiesta. Four or five parents will usually join us. The parents have a chance to see their students' interaction with me and with peers. The parents also see me as a teacher who is interested in the academic success of their students. I am willing to go beyond what is expected, and so is their student. It also gives me a chance to make a positive connection with the parents. If a problem with one of their students does arise, it is easier to contact the parent and work out a solution together.

Helpful Hints

1. Send out invitations to the Factoring Fiesta as soon as possible. Have it signed and returned as a homework assignment.

2. Have a large number of problems readily available, ranging from easy to difficult.

3. Relax. It is difficult for me to relinquish control of the class, but an open atmosphere is desired.

4. Introduce yourself to each parent and to the other parents as they enter. Make them feel welcome.

5. Don't forget plates, napkins, cups, and utensils.

Growing, Growing, GROWING!!!
A Statistical Journey

Linda E. Hains
Rock Hill, South Carolina

GRADES

10 to 12

SUBJECTS

Mathematics, science, social studies, statistics, biological and life sciences, U.S. history

OVERVIEW

In this project, students will collect the daily population figures for the world and the United States during the month of September (or any other month you wish to use). At the end of the month, we will analyze the type of graph formed and discuss the problems that can be encountered using statistical analysis.

OBJECTIVES

In this activity, students will do the following:

1. Collect population data using the Internet Census PopClock

2. Determine what type of graph best represents the growth of the world and U.S. populations

3. Determine what social, economic, and biological factors contributed to the changes in the population

4. Determine the best-fit line for the data

5. Make predictions and discuss social implications of the growth curve

MATERIALS AND RESOURCES

This activity requires the following resources:

- Microsoft *Encarta Encyclopedia*

- Census Bureau Homepage Resources: http://www.census.gov/population/www/censusdata/cencounts.html

- TI-82 graphing calculator

- TI-82 graphing overhead

- GraphLink

PROCEDURE

During the month of September, the students collect daily population figures for the United States and the world using the Internet Census PopClock. At the end of the month, we enter the data in our graphing calculators and determine what type of function best fits the data: a constant function. We discuss why this is not an accurate representation of the U.S. population. After much discussion, the students finally decide that the time frame is too short.

We then analyze the data figures for 45 years and determine that these data are linear. Once again, we discuss whether this linear model is a good representation of the population growth in our country. After we look at the way the population is predicted and the students see that people are being born at a faster rate than they are dying, the class decides that this is not an accurate graph either.

We then enter the population figures for the past 175 years. Our graph now becomes exponential. The students decide that this is the most accurate graph of the population.

Using the "trace" function of our graphing calculators, we are able to spot points where the U.S. population dropped because of historical factors such as World War II. Using Microsoft *Encarta,* students are able to find some social and economic reasons for the changes in population. After determining a line of best fit and a regression equation for our data, we can "look into the future" to the year 2050 and see that the U.S. population will be 700 million if we continue to grow exponentially. This projection enables us to discuss such issues as population density, ecologic density, and the social implications involved.

As an extension, some of my students are collecting data on the population of South Carolina to see how our growth compares with that of the U.S. population. Others are researching the implications of social policies (in various countries) such as limitations on immigration and governmental encouragement for (or prohibition of) contraception and family planning. By relating historical and biological factors to the population curve, students become motivated and eager to analyze data.

BACKGROUND

To prepare my students for the analysis required in this project, we collect small samples of data and create scatterplots. We then learn how to make prediction equations and determine regression lines. To prepare students for the research component of the project, we research several topics using Microsoft *Encarta*.

EXTENSION

This activity can also be completed using a spreadsheet with graphing capabilities such as Microsoft Excel.

CONCLUSION

After we finish the project, all my students are more aware of the dangers of making statistical predictions based on very little data. You can make the data say almost anything. The project provided my students with a sense of accomplishment as they analyzed real situations. Some of their predictions proved not to be accurate because of insufficient data points, and the students were able to determine this fact. My students especially enjoyed making the connections with science, English, and social studies.

RESOURCES

The primary resources for this project are as follows:

Microsoft *Encarta*

Internet Census PopClock

Texas Instruments graphing calculator and overhead

GraphLink

For articles, maps, or other media pertaining to this topic, look up the following in *Encarta Encyclopedia*:

Population

Population characteristics

Population control

Overpopulation

Malthus, Thomas Robert

Statistics

Zero population growth

Refer to the following items in *Encarta Interactive World Atlas* for relevant information:

World stats (population)

World themes (population growth)

For additional online information and media, view the following *Encarta* articles:

Population

Population characteristics

Population control

Statistics

For additional relevant information, visit World PopClock (http://www.census.gov/cgI-bin/ipc/popclockw): The World PopClock from the U.S. Bureau of the Census gives an estimate of the number of human beings living on the planet at the current time, as well as historical information.

Helpful Tips

1. Spend advance time going over how to enter data and graph data in the graphing calculator.

2. Create a form and assign each student a day to collect data from the Internet.

3. Don't collect data over the weekends. This makes an interesting question when you ask the students why there are gaps in the graphs.

4. Use an Overhead ViewScreen for the calculator to enable students to see the graph of the future population.

5. Investigate the errors that the population graphs can display. (Be sure to discuss time, number of data points, scale, etc.)

CHAPTER *4*

Exploring Science, Math, and Technology

T his is the place to discover how teachers are instructing science, math, and technology.

▨ Chapter Overview

- **Douglas L. Bailer,** a teacher at Pisgah High School in Pisgah, Alabama, has students as teachers, with high school students conducting a mathematics activity in an elementary classroom.

- **Shirley Newton,** a science teacher at Westerville North High School in Westerville, Ohio, explains how traditional science instruction is enhanced by a unique facility, the Science Learning Center.

- **William Ennis,** a physics teacher and science department chair at East Anchorage High School in Anchorage, Alaska, believes that of all disciplines physics is the most amenable to technology use: "It is highly mathematical and data intensive."

■ **Douglas L. Bailer,** a teacher at Pisgah High School in Pisgah, Alabama, explains how the use of entertaining anecdotes supplements the learning process.

■ **Carmen Gumina,** a biology teacher at Webster High School in Webster, New York, calls assessments "celebrations" because they celebrate newfound knowledge.

■ **Douglas L. Bailer,** a teacher at Pisgah High School in Pisgah, Alabama, uses a hands-on activity integrating math and science. He notes, "The students appreciate both the challenge and the novelty of building and actually flying a plane."

■ **Roy Coleman,** a physics teacher at Morgan Park High School in Chicago, Illinois, shares a cross-curricular lesson involving physics, mathematics, biology, reading, and writing.

▨ Students as Teachers

Douglas L. Bailer
Pisgah, Alabama

In Spring 2000, the National Council of Teachers of Mathematics (NCTM) released the much-anticipated *Principles and Standards for School Mathematics.* This book redirects and clarifies the themes presented in the NCTM's curriculum, evaluation, and professional standards documents. One of the primary thrusts held in common by both the old and new standards is that all students in Grades K-12 should have access to high-quality mathematics instruction. This instruction should include problem solving and applications of mathematics to a wide range of topics. The standards also emphasize the need for students to be able to communicate mathematics effectively both orally and in writing. I am a firm believer that one of the best ways for students to reach this high level of understanding is to require them to explain or teach mathematics to someone else.

Holding firm to this belief, six years ago I started requiring students in each of my classes to conduct a mathematics activity for a lower grade. Because Pisgah High School houses kindergarten through 12th grade on the same campus, this activity has been very simple to implement. I have found that it can also be incorporated with a great deal of success with feeder schools whose students come to us in the ninth grade. The project usually consists of two visits by my students during each semester. The first time is to present a teacher-selected lesson on a simple mathematical concept. The other time is for a student-selected lesson on an application of mathematics.

The project begins within the first few weeks of school. My students, working in small groups, are required to contact an elementary grade teacher whom I have assigned. The teachers select a concept for the high school students to present to the elementary students. The concept must be narrow enough that instruction and evaluation can be completed within a 30- to 45-minute time span.

The high school students must prepare all the material they will need to conduct the lesson and evaluate performance (handouts, overheads, etc.). After the lesson, my students are required to turn in a report that indicates their feelings about the value of the lesson to themselves and to the younger learners. In addition, the cooperating teacher completes an observation form that indicates the effectiveness of the high school student.

Once the high school students have had the experience of conducting a lesson on a topic selected by the observing teacher, they are then required to research an application of mathematics that fits into the Alabama Course of Study and to present this material to an elementary class. Though not required, students normally choose to conduct their second lesson in the same classroom. The only requirement for the second presentation is that it must be an application of mathematics that they have studied while in my class. I encourage, but do not require, my students to include in their lesson a concrete learning activity. The high school students normally complete this lesson during the last month of school. Again, students must turn in a summary report as well as the observation forms completed by the co-operating teacher.

I feel that these activities have a positive effect on the students at Pisgah High School. The older students seem to truly enjoy conducting the lessons in the elementary classrooms. In their summaries, they almost always indicate that the experience was positive. I also feel that they comprehend the mathematics they are required to teach much more than they would if they had not prepared for a presentation to a lower-grade class. The reason for this is that my students spend a great deal of time preparing their lessons, including anticipating where the younger students may experience difficulty.

Although it is true that the level of mathematics being investigated by the high school students is very low, the degree of understanding they possess after conducting these lessons is very high. This depth of understanding is more valuable to students than a breadth of knowledge over a range of topics they do not truly understand.

The significance of these activities is not limited to the high school students. In most cases, the ones who receive the greatest benefit are the elementary students. The elementary students receive from these lessons a wide range of interesting mathematical ideas. This is especially true of the application lessons. In addition to the mathematical knowledge gained, the younger students get to see the older students enjoying mathematics. This helps to motivate the elementary children to perform better in their math classes.

Such activities by high school students need not be limited to schools that include kindergarten through 12th grade. In fact, the success I had with these activities inspired me to take a group of my students to three different feeder schools. We conducted similar activities with them last year. In the spring, 30 high school students and I spent three hours at each of the elementary/junior high schools that send students to Pisgah High School. Two students and I worked with the eighth graders at the feeder schools, and the rest of my students were distributed throughout the other grades. The time was spent conducting hands-on mathematics and science activities designed to stimulate student interest.

The high school students selected and prepared all of the activities conducted. The administrators and teachers at the feeder schools were very cooperative, and I feel that we had a positive influence upon their students. These trips were such a success that my principal has agreed not only to have my students and me go again this spring but also to provide financial backing to purchase materials for the activities.

Requiring my students to complete lessons in lower grades has proved to be educationally beneficial to many student groups. Whether it is the high school students or the younger students, the lessons have had a positive effect on a majority of the students involved. In addition, the program has allowed for a great deal of cooperation between the secondary students at Pisgah High School and the elementary teachers and students.

Helpful Tips

1. Before beginning the project, spend time with your students discussing the elements of an effective lesson. Clearly define instructional objectives, multiple methods for presentation, and evaluation techniques. By doing this, not only will you help your students present a better lesson, but also you will help them clarify the significant elements of the mathematics being presented.

2. Remember to *offer* this activity as a supplement to instruction in the lower grades. Do not be disappointed if some of the teachers you approach are not interested in taking time out of their schedules for your students.

3. Use evaluation methods with your students that mirror methods used by your school system to evaluate teachers. I have the cooperating teachers fill out a form when evaluating my students'

performance. The teachers, because they are comfortable with the school system's forms, consider my forms very easy to complete.

Reference

National Council of Teachers of Mathematics. (2000). *Principles and standards for school mathematics.* Reston, VA: Author.

The Science Learning Center

Shirley Newton
Westerville, Ohio

At Westerville North High School, traditional science instruction is enhanced by a unique facility, the Science Learning Center. Facilitated by science teacher Shirley Newton, it provides a range of learning opportunities and is available to students of any academic ability level. With a focus on technology, students may learn sophisticated software applications, utilize word-processing or information presentation applications, or access means of remediation side by side with students who are conducting original research. Students compose science presentations on selected science topics with an emphasis on concepts included on the Ohio Proficiency Test (OPT). These presentations provide an outlet for creativity and self-expression as students learn to incorporate images from digital camera, scanner, video clips, and Internet resources. Involvement of staff, students, and administration has created liaisons between departments within the school and the district while also establishing community bonds. Practices that make our program available for replication are in place or planned.

Approximately 10 years ago, Westerville revised its science curriculum in an effort to make science instruction and programs more accessible and authentic for our increasingly diverse student population. To address the needs of students with a wide range of abilities and interests and to reflect a "science for all Americans" focus, our revised science curriculum included plans for the inclusion of an innovative new facility, the Science Learning Center (SLC), to operate as an adjunct to existing modes of classroom instruction and also to provide less traditional learning opportunities for our students.

Now in operation for six years, three to four classes of students each semester are enrolled in our SLC/Multimedia Production class, which confers 0.5 credits in science to those who successfully complete the course requirements. Those requirements include the construction of a multifaceted teaching tool, planned and authored by students, for use by their peers. Emphasizing interactive computer presentations (or tutorials), students in small groups plan, research, and compose these tutorials on a variety of science topics ranging from basic concepts to advanced and highly specialized areas of scientific study.

Each tutorial consists of a "homepage" that provides a menu of related subtopics. The eventual student-user of each tutorial may navigate through the presentation at his or her own pace. Each presentation includes a quiz or test that permits the user to self-evaluate new learning. A study guide requiring written responses by the user is a useful component. Authors are encouraged to make their projects attractive and appealing. Originality is encouraged and is usually evidenced in the form of original graphics, colorful pages, animations, and unique methods of enlivening the concepts presented. As students work collaboratively both within and outside their groups, peer assessment occurs constantly.

On a more formal basis, student groups display their "works in progress" to their peers at the end of each quarter and demonstrate their final products near the end of each semester. Classmate-evaluators complete a rubric providing peer assessment along with constructive suggestions for revision. Because projects are shared, technical tips and ideas are always a part of the ensuing discussions.

The philosophy of the teacher and administrator developers of this program was that interactive computer presentations, constructed by students for students, would be a practical and useful means of engaging those who might be unsuccessful in the traditional science classroom setting. Students requiring remediation are identified by their ninth-grade OPT scores. Over the course of three school years, we have had one class per semester and one class each summer available to those students who have not yet passed the science portion of the OPT. Teachers of the classes have used the SLC-constructed presentations as instructional tools and indicate a high degree of student involvement when using them. Although the student-authored tutorials are one of many instructional methods used by these teachers, a proficiency test passing rate averaging 20% has resulted each semester among those students enrolled in our remediation classes.

Students in the remediation classes are also given online assignments, using the SLC computers, with the intention of improving their computer skills, demonstrating the value of using the Internet as a learning tool and information resource, and as an alternative to traditional teacher-directed instruction. In many instances, students who have yet to pass the science portion of the ninth-grade OPT have elected to enroll in SLC/Multimedia Production and have participated in construction of a tutorial coordinating with an area or areas in which their test scores indicate the need for remediation. The majority of those students have since passed the OPT.

As the SLC program has evolved, some SLC/Multimedia Production students have opted to become involved in production of science presentations in topic areas other than the very basic. For example, an ecology teacher engaged SLC students in the construction of a Web site for a local group of environmentalists, Friends of Alum Creek. Another ecology teacher is working with students who are authoring a presentation on Westerville North's Field Studies program with special emphasis on Ohio's snake populations. A chemistry teacher has asked a pair of SLC students to construct a presentation on combustion that he intends to use as an instructional tool when he discusses reaction types with his chemistry classes. Frequent interaction between teachers "contracting" these projects takes place on an informal basis. This interaction is an evaluative tool that is practical and authentic.

The tailor-made presentations provide the authors an opportunity to construct a practical tool with an intended end-user whose input communicates specific needs and goals, paralleling real-world work situations. Students are motivated to improve their computer skills in an effort to construct a product that will be both appealing and instructionally sound.

Multimedia projects are graded using a comprehensive rubric that evaluates accuracy and thoroughness of concepts presented, evidence of mastery of software applications, and inclusion of required components of a complete "package." Additionally, an open-ended evaluation of the program is completed by student-producers. For example, students were asked if focusing on one topic for an entire semester increased their knowledge in that area. A typical response was this:

My partner and I focused on tree botany, an Advanced Biology course topic taught at WNHS. We worked with our teacher to create an informative program to assist students/teacher with learning this subject. Completing this project reinforced what we learned during the course and helped us to become experts.

In response to the same question, a student who completed a project on chemical reactions wrote, "I feel that I learned a lot more about it in this class than I would have in any chemistry class."

When asked to describe the unique aspects of the SLC class, one student said,

No other class works like SLC to improve a student's relationship with technology. This unique experience is crucial for preparing students for the future. Also, by being in an open learning environment, students can focus on featuring their creative skills.

Another said, "This class is unique because you can learn skills to any extent. Once you learn the basics, you can take it upon yourself to go beyond the normal level and really master a skill."

Students were asked whether completion of the SLC/Multimedia Production class would be of value to them in the future. A student who composed a tutorial on quantum mechanics and one on relativity replied, "I learned to do research efficiently on a specific topic that I needed to learn about." Another said, "Obviously the future is computers. By taking this class I have a head start over everyone that is starting from scratch."

Typical responses regarding whether experiences working with another student improved communication skills and enhanced one's ability to work with others on a project included the following:

In a project as elaborate as ours, it is absolutely necessary to have good communication skills and to be able to work with others. The demands of this particular assignment improved my communication skills and enhanced my ability to function as a productive team member.

These quotes confirm that the student authors in the Multimedia Production classes learn and improve while creating an authentic product that will have practical application benefiting teachers and other students.

Planned, but not yet in place, is the inclusion of some of our tutorials, especially those on topics specifically addressing OPT objectives, on the school Web site. Macromedia Director files may be saved as Shockwave files that are accessible via the Internet. In this manner, the student authors' projects not only would be showcased publicly but also could be accessed by any student, of any age, seeking remediation in basic science concepts.

Additionally, Westerville North High School has video conferencing capability, accommodated by a dedicated T1 line. An auxiliary computer is used to transmit computer files to another site. A future goal is to link with other schools, enabling SLC students to discuss construction of their projects, to discuss the particulars of using the software, or to assist those needing remediation by presenting their tutorials.

An obvious confirmation of our adherence to the Ohio Department of Education's priorities of higher standards, rigorous assessments, and improved performance came when one of our student-authored tutorials, "Waves," created by three SLC/Multimedia Production students, was selected as national winner, high school division, by the sponsors of Multimedia Mania. The three students along with their teacher-facilitator were treated to an expenses-paid three-day trip to San Diego to receive the award and to present the winning project to an audience of educators from around the world. A press release from the Web site www.sasinschool read as follows:

> Press Releases Winners of Multimedia Mania contest announced SAN DIEGO, Calif. (June 22, 1998)—Winners of Multimedia Mania, an international multimedia contest for students, were announced today at the 1998 National Educational Computing Conference (NECC) in San Diego, Calif. Teachers of the winning student teams . . . and Shirley Newton of Westerville North High School, Westerville, Ohio. In a keynote session at NECC on Wednesday, June 25, winners will receive an award plaque and present their projects, which demonstrate how technology can be used to teach standard curricula. The

purpose of Multimedia Mania is to have students develop multi-media projects that answer the question, "Does technology have a positive impact on learning?" Projects were judged on the basis of instructional design, content subject knowledge, graphical design, mechanics, screen design, and use of video or 3-D modeling. In evaluating projects, an international panel of judges placed strong emphasis on curriculum standards and the creative use of technology to address a standard course of study. Student winners and their teacher received free software and a trip to NECC to present their projects.

As a direct result of this accomplishment, the three SLC students who authored the presentation and won the contest were invited to present at the SchoolTech Expo in New York City in March 1999. They participated in a three-hour Interactive Classroom in which teachers and students conducted simulated classroom interactions and answered questions posed by conference attendees.

One of the Improvement Priorities Goals, as listed on the Ohio Department of Education's Web site, is that "Ohio schools will have the capacity and community support to reach high academic performance." Linking to the community by establishing partnerships and tapping into resources outside of the school's walls conforms to that goal. Several students in the SLC are currently constructing interactive presentations that will be included on the TeensLook@Health page that will be accessed from the www. Netwellness.org Web site, a project sponsored by three Ohio medical schools including that of Ohio State University.

Creating projects on health-related topics such as smoking cessation, breast cancer, fitness, and nutrition, each student group is researching, planning, and constructing a presentation that reflects our SLC's philosophy that student-authored informational presentations will be of special interest and therefore will be more likely to be used by teens. Each group has been paired with a medical student from Ohio

State University who is assessing the information and assisting in revisions. Input from the medical students is intended to ensure that information is accurate and current. Endorsed by Ohio SchoolNet, a NetWellness representative is meeting with our students weekly.

Several SLC students have been, and are, participating in an inter-departmental project that combines several departments, including English, Economics, School-to-Work, and Work and Family Life, in a business partnership with our Adopt-a-School partner Cheryl & Co., located in Westerville. SLC students served as scientific advisers to Foods class members as they tested and developed a unique cookie. SLC students also recorded major events using digital and video cameras and compiled a "scrapbook" of the project. That digital scrapbook has been used extensively by the School-to-Work coordinator in presentations throughout the state. SLC students designed the logo for the project, the Scholar Snack, and assisted in the marketing and promotion of the product.

During the current school year, SLC students have assisted in the development of a second cookie flavor and have designed the product label. They have spoken personally to a representative of Lyons Data, our printer, regarding the conversion of our computer-created logo to print. CCHIP (Cheryl & Co. Hometown Integrated Project) was a 1999 recipient of a BEST Practices Award. Last year's profit of approximately $1,400 was distributed, in the form of academic "scholarcchips", to three graduating seniors who had been active in CCHIP. This year, we anticipate substantially increased profits and will increase scholarships to student participants.

Westerville North teachers participated in the construction of the COOL (Connections Offered OnLine) Web site, sponsored by Ohio SchoolNet and available for viewing at www.ohioschoolnet.k12.oh. us/cool. The Web site features eight innovative projects that link schools with businesses, government agencies, zoos, or museums. Clicking on the "Industry" icon provides suggestions for planning a project similar to our CCHIP, contacting prospective business partners, implementing the project, assessing learning outcomes, and extending learning opportunities.

Submitted but not yet available from the SchoolNet Web site is a detailed Lesson Lab featuring all of the steps in our project, from its inception through the development and marketing of our chocolate chip cookie. Also included are photos of many of the activities associated with our project, as well as specific class assignments and assessment tools that were used by the our team's teachers. E-mail addresses are included on the site allowing interested educators worldwide to contact us for assistance in adapting our project to their needs.

Obviously, these and similar accomplishments and innovative projects depend upon the guidance and support of staff and administrators. With a focus on enhancing educational opportunities for students, participation in special projects requires expenditures of time and energy far in excess of the typical. Creation of a "learning culture" that advances the knowledge and experiences of both students and staff are encouraged with few, if any, restrictions on the parts of administrators and supervisors.

For schools that may be considering a similar program, we encourage you to implement a multimedia production facility in small steps. Our program began with the purchase of a few computers, appropriate software, and minimal peripherals such as a digital camera. Recruitment of a few students, working closely with a teacher while learning the software and developing curricular goals, is a good start. As projects are created that represent these goals, commitments to staffing, equipping, and finding appropriate space for the facility are likely to be forthcoming.

To the class facilitator, don't underestimate students' abilities. Remain open to learning *from* the students. Many of them are extremely adept, having been raised in the midst of our technology-centered culture. Their creativity and motivation to advance their abilities are incredible. Take advantage. Encourage collaboration among students. Create opportunities for them to view others' work and to share "tips and tricks" as well as constructive criticisms. Finally, support creative expression, but set limits. For example, presentations must adhere to the school's policies regarding references to illegal substances, inappropriate sexual references, or profanity. Emphasizing that their final products will be displayed to a wide audience, including adults and possibly administrators or community members, helps in that regard.

▧ Physics and Technology

William Ennis
Anchorage, Alaska

Technology is the servant, albeit a powerful one, of the modern science classroom. In my physics and advanced placement physics classes, we use technology whenever it is appropriate. For the most part, we use technology to acquire and analyze data and to model physical interactions. My classes use data acquisition devices to take rapid and accurate measurements during labs. These data are uploaded to computers for analysis. After analysis, students use computers to create reports. Modeling software is used to enhance student understanding of physical concepts, and it sometimes replaces real-world lab exercises when effects (friction, predominantly) obscure the target phenomena.

Of all disciplines, physics is the most amenable to technology use. It is highly mathematical and data intensive. Additionally, it is easy to incorporate Alaska State Standards for mathematics because these performance standards include specific mention of creating and understanding graphs, understanding mathematical relationships, and using a graphing calculator. The Technology section of Alaska's Content Standards for Students might have been written for a physics class. The standards mention mastery of skills such as troubleshooting; using technology to observe, analyze, interpret, and draw conclusions; and solving problems both individually and with others. It sounds like a physics lab!

The beauty of our advanced technology is that it enables students to take more data in a class period than was possible in several days using more traditional methods. Gathering accurate data quickly affords gathering more data and having time for extensive analysis. It is, after all, the patterns in the data that make data important. For students to see a parabola in data that they have gathered is an epiphany. For most students, this is their first opportunity to wonder at the mystical similarity of structure that mathematics and nature share.

Traditionally, high school physics begins with a study of kinematics, Galileo's science of motion. Students are introduced to this topic through a series of lessons that gives them an understanding of graph interpretation, generation of equations from data, linear regression, and basic kinematics. These lessons incorporate short labs and traditional classroom techniques. After mastery of these preliminary concepts and skills, we are ready for the Galileo Lab, in which students perform an exhaustive set of trials of a ball rolling down inclined planes set at various angles.

Students are also required and encouraged to use computer simulation software. With this newly available resource, students are able to completely control a simulated laboratory. They can modify or eliminate the effects of air resistance, gravity, and friction (among other effects). They are encouraged to build their intuition for the physical situation that we will use in the lab by changing ramp angles, gravitational acceleration, and friction. The freedom to manipulate a world is captivating, and students respond with enthusiasm. Often, individual students and groups of students return to "play" with the modeling software after school.

The lab itself is a multiday affair. Students must go to Web sites to download the particular software needed for the experiment. They must load the software into their calculators and debug the systems before they can even begin to take data. This stage can be frustrating to students without computer skills, but the smiles that occur when the first data are taken make the effort worthwhile. Students will be using the same technology for many labs, so mastery now will pay dividends throughout the year.

Lab data include position-versus-time data for five ramp angles. As a volleyball or other ball rolls down a ramp, the motion detectors generate mountains of data. These data are analyzed with a view toward proving with the data that motion on the ramp is accelerated by proving that it complies with a formal definition of acceleration.

Normally, student lab groups are given a full week in which to produce the lab report. The formal report is many typed pages in length and includes many graphs, all produced on computer. To the dismay of some students (and to the delight of English teachers!), punctuation, spelling, and writing are also graded. Organization of the data within the report is also important.

Internet Site

Texas Instruments (TI) Web site: http://www.ti.com/calc/docs/calchome.html

Equipment and Software

TI CBL and motion detector

TI GraphLink

Interactive Physics, a software product published by MSC Software (Web site at http://www.workingmodel.com/products/ip.html).

Helpful Tips

1. Encourage the students to create their own lab groups.

2. Provide an example of a good lab report for their use. Many students have never been required to produce a lab report and have only completed a lab sheet.

3. Consider a joint project with English teachers for which students might gain credit for their work. Collaboration with other departments is usually welcomed. Let students fret a little! The world will pay these students for their ability to make things work. If they have never had to troubleshoot an apparatus, now is the time.

4. Provide only schematic directions. Encourage students to create solutions themselves. Don't do all their thinking for them.

5. Request that advanced students attend class as helpers the first day. Students teaching students is usually a good thing.

Educational Stories

Douglas L. Bailer
Pisgah, Alabama

There is no doubt that students growing up during the last part of the 20th century have been bombarded with a vast array of technological inventions. Because of the preponderance of new gadgets in their lives, modern-day students are extremely comfortable using technology. This fact has led many educators across the country to believe that most, if not all, of a student's educational career should be spent in front of a computer screen. These "techno-educators" seem to think that the best way to educate students in the 21st century is with a personal computer, a television, and an "educational program." Although technology is beneficial in a great many ways, the key to effective instruction in any subject area is as old as the spoken word. A good, well-developed educational story will go farther in helping a student learn than all of the computing power in the world. By educational storytelling, I mean the use of entertaining anecdotes to supplement the learning process.

The first and most crucial element to creating an effective educational story is a clearly defined educational objective. A good educational story is very specific in the learning outcomes students should be able to demonstrate after hearing it. Therefore it is not a good idea to teach large blocks of study using stories that develop and turn into educational novels. It is important that the story be short, clear, and focused on one or two learning goals.

The second rule to remember when constructing a good educational story is to link the theme of the story to the students' previous knowledge. Students should not be required to learn new characters or tie together intricate details while learning via the use of educational stories. An effective story will get its message across in much the same way as a joke: subtly. Teachers should therefore avoid introducing a lot of elements to the story that are not related to the learning goals. The key concept here is to keep the story simple and allow it to develop from the learning goal rather than the other way around.

Once the goals have been established and the teacher assesses the prior knowledge of the students, the story can then be developed. A good starting place for novices in the art of education via storytelling is with acronyms. An example of the use of acronyms can be demonstrated in the study of right triangles. All math teachers have heard SOHCAHTOA used as a way of recalling the relationships that exist between the sides of a triangle as expressed by the three basic trigonometric functions. The SOH helps students remember that sine x = opposite side ÷ hypotenuse. CAH reminds students that cosine x = adjacent side ÷ hypotenuse. The final syllable, TOA, helps students recall that tangent x = opposite side ÷ adjacent side. I have carried this simple acronym to a higher level by the development of the story of "Chief Sohcahtoa." The story uses Chief Sohcahtoa's teepee as its main element. This teepee is, of course, a right triangle. I use several small jokes to relate the sides of the teepee to the chief's name and thus to the three trigonometric functions. Students find it very easy to remember the six basic trigonometric functions as applied to the right triangle because they enjoy the story of Chief Sohcahtoa.

Although the learning goals in the story of Chief Sohcahtoa are specific, the story itself is fairly long. This need not be the case for all educational stories. The application of one-liners can be an effective way of helping students learn. One of the most effective ways I have applied this type of story is in the teaching of element symbols in chemistry. As I am introducing the elements that I want my students to know the symbols of, I do not simply give them a list and say "Learn the symbols for these elements." Instead, I make up a joke to help students remember the one or two letters that make up each element's symbol. Here are a few examples:

1. The chemical symbol for sodium is Na. Most students know that salt is sodium chloride (though they don't know that the symbol is NaCl). So I tell my students that the next time they go to the lunchroom, they should say to the manager "Na, I don't want any salt."

2. The chemical symbol for copper is Cu. There is a police officer, named Officer Davis, who is well known and well liked by almost all of my students. I tell my students that the next time they see Officer Davis leaving campus, they should yell "See you (Cu) copper."

3. The chemical symbol for gold is Au. Auburn University (AU) is one of the two major universities in Alabama, the other being the University of Alabama. Because of the intense rivalry between the two, students tend to either love Auburn or hate it. Therefore I tell my students that when they think of AU (Au), they can either think of gold or fool's gold—either way, they remember that Au is gold.

Throughout the process, I encourage students to help me create the anecdotes for each element. In fact, the one for Au being gold was created by a couple of Auburn fans last year. Of course, an Alabama fan chirped in with "fool's gold" in the next second, and a very effective teaching strategy was born. These simple-to-create one-liners have helped transform educational drudgery into an entertaining experience that is fun for both the students and myself.

There are multitudes of other ways to incorporate stories into the educational environment. These strategies could include singing to students or using role play. Though not a true story, the use of songs or role play can be an effective way of incorporating entertainment into the educational schema of a teacher's classroom. I know teachers who sing to their students and get wonderful results.

I personally prefer to combine these two activities by directing my students in an occasional song and dance. A good example of this is my yearly "matrix shuffle." Students perform a simple song-and-dance routine while learning the elementary elements of matrices. I give the students the basic idea and encourage them to create their own words and motions. This activity is both entertaining and educationally beneficial.

Technology is great and is essential for the completion of some aspects of my job; however, as far as my teaching responsibilities are concerned, I find that technology plays second fiddle to old-fashioned storytelling. Regardless of the way educational stories are implemented in my classroom, they almost certainly help liven up the learning process.

Helpful Tips

1. Remember that you are a human—you make mistakes. If you let your students see you as human, they will respond to your educational stories in a more receptive manner.

2. Start with simple ideas and let your storytelling develop at its own pace. You will find that even when you think a story is complete, there will be room for improvements.

The "Peer Celebration"

Carmen Gumina
Webster, New York

The students in my classroom are involved in many group activities, and my favorite one is the "Peer Celebration." We don't have "tests" in our classroom—too many kids have "test anxiety," and God forbid I should add any more stress to their lives. So we call our assessments "celebrations" because we are celebrating our newfound knowledge . . . and it's tough to get nervous about a celebration.

Now our celebrations sometimes take the form of the traditional New York State science assessment—multiple choice and essay. But at least once a quarter my students are randomly placed in groups of three or four, and they take a Peer Celebration. They are given the exam questions (about 15 to 20) about five days ahead of time, and their common goal is to research each question to determine the correct answer. I expect each team to get nearly all the answers correct, but the fun part comes when they are held responsible for the incorrect choices as well.

On the day of our Peer Celebration (which usually follows one or two days of in-class research), I randomly call on a particular group to explain one of the questions. Those in that group have 30 seconds to look over their notes and determine the role of each person. They then stand up, put away their notes, read the question to their classmates, and state the correct answer. Each team member then explains in detail why the other three or four choices are incorrect (they have 90 to 120 seconds to complete this step). At the end of the explanations, I ask them if they'd like to supplement any of their teammates' statements (e.g., perhaps someone wasn't as clear as they could be, or perhaps one of them said something that was inaccurate).

After this "supplemental period" (usually about 15 to 30 seconds), I ask those on the team questions about their rationale—this lets me know whether or not they truly understand what they've just presented. Keep in mind that once a team stands up, its members cannot refer back to their notes—they have to really know and understand their material in order to maximize their score. I also tell them that they can use the overhead, chalkboard, whiteboard, and so forth to get their point across. After the group has completed its explanations, I quickly call on the next group.

Points are awarded as follows: three points for the correct answer and four to seven points for each explanation (depending on how clear and accurate the explanation is). Each team will be asked three questions from the test packet throughout the class period.

The students would all tell you that this type of assessment is much more work but that they get so much more from it. In a way, they become teachers to each of their teammates and also to the rest of their classmates. My favorite part of this activity is listening to the students "discuss science" during their in-class research. They help each other understand different points of view. They go to their textbooks and notebooks to get facts that will bolster their arguments. I have to believe that the effort is so much more intense than if they were just preparing for one of our traditional exams. To hear them defend their reasoning to each other is the true assessment—they can't help but succeed when they finally stand up to explain their choices.

This year I've followed this activity up with a "solo celebration," which includes some of the same questions they've already worked on in groups. The average scores are significantly higher when compared to other exams that were not coupled with this type of peer activity.

This type of activity has been successful with all three levels of biology that I teach (general, regents, advanced placement), but it does take some additional class time, especially with the general and regents classes. The advanced placement students will get together after school to work on their questions, but this hasn't been the case with my other classes, so I dedicate two class days (40-minute periods) to research, and my regents students are strongly urged to spend one of their common study hall periods to tie up any loose ends.

Because of these time constraints, I only plan on one peer exam per quarter. An added benefit, however, is that this type of activity doesn't lose its charm and sense of novelty with the students.

Helpful Tips

1. It takes two to three minutes per group to get through a question.

2. I try not to answer too many questions during the in-class research sessions that precede the peer exam.

3. I don't give more than 20 questions to be researched. This is the maximum number that I've found students can get researched in two 40-minute periods.

4. I tell the students that everyone in the group gets the same grade—obviously I make exceptions for someone who is noticeably strong or weak during the explanations.

Building and Flying Remote-Controlled Model Airplanes

Douglas L. Bailer
Pisgah, Alabama

In 1996, the Alabama State Department of Education (ASDE) enacted new high school graduation requirements that are among the most stringent in the nation. Not only do the new graduation standards require students to take more difficult coursework in mathematics and science, but also it is mandatory that all students pass a comprehensive battery of graduation exams. The science and mathematics graduation exams require students to demonstrate competency in Algebra I, general chemistry, and introductory physics. Although I applaud the ASDE for the lofty goals set forth in their 1996 decision, these new graduation requirements have meant changes in the way teachers approach mathematics and science instruction. One of the most beneficial tactics being used at Pisgah High School is the integration of mathematics and science through hands-on activities. By far, the most successful of these activities has been the construction and flying of remote-controlled model airplanes.

This project has been used in both general physics and applied mathematics classes. Because of the great amount of time required, the planes are constructed as an ongoing project. Pisgah High School is on a 96-minute block schedule. I find this class length very beneficial for this type of project. Students work on the planes for 15 to 20 minutes a day. Depending on the complexity of the plane and the aptitude of the students, the project can last from 9 to 18 weeks. The students appreciate both the challenge and the novelty of building and actually flying a plane.

The first step in the process of constructing the planes is the selection of an appropriate kit. Teachers who are novices to remote-controlled aircraft will discover very quickly that there is a vast array of supplies on the market, most of which are not suitable for high school students. An ideal situation for teachers planning to start this type of project would be for them to enlist the aid of a local hobby supply store for the selection of planes and building equipment. If no such hobby store exists in the area, teachers can find national hobby supply stores online or through model magazines. The main caution to this type of plane selection is that teachers should avoid "good buys" in lieu of planes that come with really good instructions. In fact, it would not be unreasonable for a teacher who is considering investing $500 per plane to ask for and receive sample instruction packets from manufacturing companies. Other things to look for in a high-quality plane kit include laser-cut parts (they will fit together much more easily) and an ample accessory package. Anything not included in the accessory package has to be purchased separately. Manufacturers can inform teachers of the items needed to complete the plane kit.

In addition to the plane itself, teachers need to purchase an engine and radio for each plane. Because these are the only parts of the plane(s) that are reusable, teachers should consider purchasing the best radio(s) and engine(s) possible. Bargain-basement parts might save a few dollars the first year, but quality components will pay for themselves in the long run. One other important thing to remember about the radio is to purchase one with only four channels. Although there are radios available with up to eight channels, four channels will give full aerodynamic control. The extra channels are useful only if teachers are planning to add retractable landing gear or other frivolous attachments.

The final items needed before the project can begin are the building supplies. The most basic of these is a building board. A good building board can be constructed by overlaying 3/4-inch plywood with a layer of ridged foam insulation. The building board should be just large enough for the wing and fuselage to be placed on. For most planes, a piece of plywood three feet by four feet in dimension will suffice. Other building supplies that are required include CA glue, epoxy, T-pins, and a large supply of sandpaper. Other items that can prove to be useful include a hand-held drill and a scroll saw.

The airplane project begins with a unit of study on aviation. This unit focuses on knowing airplane parts, flight fundamentals, and aviation careers. This typically lasts two weeks. Teachers can receive free educational aids for developing their own aviation unit by contacting the Federal Aviation Administration (FAA), the Civil Air Patrol, and the National Aeronautics and Space Administration (NASA). The bookwork precedes the actual construction for two very important reasons. First, this unit ensures that the students know the parts of an airplane. Second, it serves as a motivational tool that stimulates student interest in the project.

During the construction process, students are introduced to a wide array of mathematics and science topics. The most obvious of these is making measurements. Because certain parts of the planes are manufactured in the United States and other parts are manufactured overseas, students must be able to measure in both standard and metric units. They must also be able to convert between the two systems of measurement. In addition, students have opportunities to practice skills from geometry while building the airplanes. In order to put the covering material over the skeleton of the planes, calculations must be made pertaining to the surface area to be covered. Throughout the building process, angular measurements and cuts are required.

The students must also demonstrate competence in a wide range of physical science topics. They have to calculate the surface area of the arc cut by the propeller and to determine the volume of air that will pass over the wing during a given number of revolutions. While considering how much air flows over the wing during a given time period, students are introduced to Bernoulli's Principle. By using inexpensive spring scales coupled with a few elementary physics formulas, students determine the lift coefficient of the wings. Teachers will find that other interesting areas of discussion will develop throughout the project.

The most significant impact this activity has had on student learning is an improvement in attitude. All teachers can attest to how important student attitude is to achievement. In the two years I have used this activity, I have not had any students express that they did not enjoy the project. In fact, most students at some time or another have expressed an appreciation for the project. This is not to say that all students have loved the idea of building a plane at school. In fact, each year several began the project with some trepidation because they feared the embarrassment that their plane would not fly. Each of these students, however, learned that planes are not complicated. The students gained a great deal of personal satisfaction from seeing their planes go up, up, and away.

Although not directly related to the building of the planes, students do have chances to use other math and science skills during this unit of study. This application of skills is accomplished by requiring my students to complete the FAA's General Aviation Unit (available free of charge from the FAA) during the construction process. This unit includes 25 task cards, each of which addresses a different aspect of aviation. The task cards make the unit interdisciplinary because the students are required to complete activities in fields of study outside mathematics or science and then use this knowledge to do a math- or science-related skill.

An example of the type of activity students complete from a task card is writing a business letter to an aircraft manufacturer. The students must identify themselves as working on an aerospace unit of study and then solicit information about a particular aircraft. The type of information the students obtain includes such items as fuel capacity and consumption and normal operating speed. Students are then required to answer questions using the formula distance = rate × time. These same data are then applied to geography skills by having students calculate the time needed to travel between two locations in the particular aircraft they selected.

The model airplane construction project has been very beneficial to student learning at Pisgah High School. Students enjoy completing the planes, and they enjoy the positive attention they receive on the days the planes are flown. Although the project requires a great deal of teacher effort, the gains in both mathematical and scientific skill coupled with the improvement in student attitude make it well worth the trouble.

Helpful Tips

1. Because the cost per plane is almost $500, my school formed a partnership with several local businesses. Under this partnership, each business provides partial financial support for one plane. In return, they get to select the color and pattern design of the plane. In addition, when the project is over, the business is given the plane (without the radio and engine). The new

owners can display the planes within their businesses. Not only does this help the school out financially, it builds a sense of connection between the school and the business community.

2. To successfully complete the project, novices to remote-controlled aircraft will find the aid of experienced builders and flyers invaluable. In most parts of the country, there is a local remote-controlled airplane club with members who would be willing and able to assist—especially for a school project.

3. The ideal group size for this project is five students per plane. This would have one student serving as leader, two students responsible for the fuselage, and two students responsible for the wings.

4. This project can be enhanced to be a math/science/social studies unit by requiring the students to construct historical aircraft. A good place to start is to research and build a model of an aircraft that fought in World War II.

▧ Determining the Brain's Processing Time Using Two Different Methods

Roy Coleman
Chicago, Illinois

This is a cross-curricular lesson involving physics, mathematics, biology, reading, and writing (Illinois Science Goals: 11B [2] and 11C [1, 3-6] on experimentation).

Purpose: To determine your brain's processing speed

Equipment: Meter stick, paper, calculator, brain, body, 4 meters of rubber tubing, two small funnels (to fit in tubing)

Today's experiment will involve the following: You will be required to find the processing time for your brain by two different methods and to compare the results. In other words, how fast does your brain function, if at all?

Part I

To do the first part of this experiment, you need to find your reaction time. This is done by placing your hand on the edge of the table and having your partner drop a ruler between your fingers as you try to catch it. Start with your fingers even with the zero mark on the ruler, and after the drop, read and record the position where you caught it (in a clearly labeled data table). At least 10 valid trials are necessary. (Remember to record *all* data, and cross off anything that is in error—don't just leave it off.) Now, using the equation for uniformly accelerated motion ($S_f = 1/2_a \Delta t^2 + V_o \Delta t + S_o$ where V_o and S_o are zero), substitute in the distance and find the reaction time. Be sure you use the average for the 10 trials.

The reaction time (t_r) consists of three parts. These are the processing time (t_p), the nerve time (t_n), and the dynamic time (t_d). Mathematically, it should be written as follows: $t_r = t_p + t_n + t_d$. The processing time is what you are looking for.

Nerve time refers to the time that is necessary for the signal from the brain to travel to the fingers. If you measure the distance from the back of the head to the middle of the back and then from the middle of the back to the end of the fingers, you will have the distance of travel. Because for most people the speed of the nerve signal (V_n) is about 300 m/s, you can use the appropriate equation to find the travel time for the nerve signal (i.e., solve $S = V_n \Delta t$ for Δt, which is t_n).

The dynamic time consists of finding how long it takes for your fingers to close. To find your dynamic time, open and close your fingers as many times as possible in 10 seconds. This gives you the number of pinches in 10 seconds. Because one pinch refers to an opening *and* a closing, you really want to find the time per half pinch, so you should double the number of full pinches. By dividing the time by the number of half pinches, you determine the dynamic time (t_d).

Now that you have the reaction time (t_r), nerve time (t_n), and dynamic time (t_d), you should be able to find the processing time (t_p).

Part II

The second part of this experiment attempts to find the processing time directly along with demonstrating a couple of other physiological properties of the human brain.

Fold the tubing in half lengthwise and mark the midpoint. Then place a funnel in each end of the tubing and have a member of the group hold a funnel over each ear. With the tubing looped behind the student, tap the tubing 30 to 50 centimeters off center from the middle mark. Have the student indicate which side he or she hears the sound coming from. Repeat the same tapping on the other side. Now tap at the center. The student should indicate that it is about in the center. Slowly tap while moving out from the center until the student can tell which side the sound is coming from. Mark that point on the tubing. Repeat the tapping on the other side and mark that side. The distance between these two points can be called a "dead spot" because the student cannot differentiate between the arrival times of the two sounds.

The marks will not be symmetrical about the center line. This is because the audio processing center of the brain is off to one side. The amount of offset is proportional to the differential in the times needed for the audio/nerve signal to reach the processing center. The time that it takes sound to travel the length of the dead spot is approximately the processing time of the brain. Knowing that sound travels through air at about 340 m/s, the processing time can be calculated by solving $\Delta S = V_s \Delta t$ for Δt (which is t_p).

You are to include in the write-up an introduction and purpose statement (a short paragraph detailing what you will determine), a data table, sample calculations, results, and a conclusion.

Helpful Tips

For Part I

The one major error that students typically make is to "follow" the ruler down when it is dropped. To counteract this natural reaction, I have the student who is catching the ruler rest his or her hand on the edge of a table so that it cannot move down.

Another problem is anticipation. This can be countered by occasionally pulling the ruler away rather than dropping it.

If the "pinch rate" seems slow, have the students wait a couple of minutes to try it again. They may have been practicing and may have tired out their finger muscles.

Typical data are as follows:

- The average distance dropped before catching should be in the 15 to 25 centimeters range, so the average reaction time should be around 0.20 seconds.

- An average student is about 1.2 meters from head to fingers, giving a nerve time of about 0.004 seconds.

- Most people can produce 30 to 40 pinches per 10 seconds, for a dynamic time of about 0.14 seconds.

If a student calculates a negative processing time, either there has been an error in his or her calculations or measurements or that student has precognition and can predict the future.

For Part II

The loop should be behind the student to keep him or her from seeing which side is being tapped on.

Typical "dead zone" distances are 30 to 40 centimeters, with an offset of about 10 to 15 centimeters. Note that this offset is about the difference in distance between the right ear to the audio processing center and the left ear to the audio processing center because the speed of sound is about the same as the speed of the nerve signals.

Done carefully, both parts should produce results for the processing time on the order of 0.01 to 0.001 seconds.

CHAPTER 5

Threading Technology Through the Curriculum

T his chapter illustrates how teachers thread technology through the curriculum.

grades, get extra help, research the library, listen to radio stations, read newspapers, download worksheets, and visit a variety of sites."

▧ Living Textbook Project

Linda E. Hains
Rock Hill, South Carolina

Objective

Students (in teams) will create a dialogue story in Microsoft Word that would be appropriate for middle and high school students on the dangers of smoking. The students will be the actors in their stories. The scenes will involve students using or trying to purchase tobacco products (all tobacco usage will be alluded to, not actually done). The scenes will be written in book form, with digital images created on the digital camera for illustrations.

The story must be written with dialogue and have a satisfactory conclusion that summarizes the reasons for not using tobacco products. The finished images will be inserted into PowerPoint presentations and given to local schools. Each school will receive a book containing the best stories and a CD (created by our students) on the dangers of teen smoking. In addition, when we study Web page creation, our students will create Web pages containing the best stories for our school Web page.

Curriculum Rationale

This project closely aligns with the state technology curriculum by creating real-life experiences for students on the use of Microsoft Word, PowerPoint, word wrap, graphics, tables, digital cameras, and Web page creation. The "Living Textbook" project challenged my students to be creative and to produce materials for educating middle and high school students about the dangers of smoking. In addition, the students felt a sense of community involvement by creating stories from a teen's perspective that might stop another teen from smoking. The Rock Hill District 3 Substance Abuse Education Program, the Rock Hill Foundation, and the York County Tobacco/Drug Prevention Partnership provided funding for the project.

A group of our students will present personal copies of the best projects to local schools in our district. Based on the quality of the projects, the materials may be distributed for smoking awareness throughout the state. By creating the smoking awareness project, my students developed a sense of creating something worthwhile in their lives and the lives of other teens.

Procedure

The group's work involved creating dialogue stories on the dangers of teen smoking. They took pictures with a digital camera of teens using tobacco products (simulated). Next, the students researched the dangers associated with teen smoking using the Internet and pamphlets from the American Cancer Association. Then they wrote dialogue stories based on their experiences with smoking. After the students wrote the stories, they created PowerPoint presentations highlighting the main points. The PowerPoint presentations helped make the information more interesting and motivational for other teens.

When my class started this project, we never dreamed that this project would take so much time and would involve us emotionally. Most of the students either had friends or parents who smoked or had been smokers themselves. As the groups gathered facts on the dangers of teen smoking, they discovered that 90% of new smokers are teens and that one third of them will die from smoking-related illnesses.

When the class finished their work, they realized that more teens must hear the truth about smoking. They wanted their friends to know IT'S OK NOT TO SMOKE! Adults write most of the materials on the dangers of teen smoking, and many of these materials are ignored by teens. The class thought that their message, written by teens for teens, would have a greater impact on the teen smoking problem. At that time, our little smoking prevention project became a Living Textbook. The class wanted as many teens as possible to read the materials and make the right decision concerning smoking.

Computer Skills Required

The students used the word-processing skills of text wrap, watermarks, Word Art, borders/shading, callout boxes, footers, tables, and inserting/editing digital pictures. By encouraging my students to create personal dialogue stories that were meaningful and current, I was able to make word processing more interesting for them.

The students used the PowerPoint skills of making transitions, building effects, inserting sound, creating animations, inserting digital pictures, and creating background effects to display the major issues involved in teen smoking using a dynamic medium. Our unit on presentations became a real-life experience instead of just another technology concept in the textbook.

The students "burned" CD-ROMs of the Living Textbook. This technology enabled us to share our project with other schools in our district and state.

Future Goals

Based on the quality of the Living Textbook, a group of my students was asked to speak before the State House and Ways Committee on the importance of teen smoking prevention programs. Our state is deciding how to distribute the tobacco settlement money. My students want a large portion ($23 million) to be spent on teen prevention programs such as the Living Textbook. The most important lesson learned by the students was that one person could make a difference in a teen's life.

Our group plans to further our project in the coming year by doing several things. One thing we want to do is produce more Living Textbooks. We would like all schools to have their own copies. Then those students can add their own stories and PowerPoint presentations to the book. Another goal for next year is to get more students involved in the project. With more students writing and producing PowerPoint presentations, their additional views and insights will improve the project.

Another thought we have for next year is making one of the stories into a play that we could show to schools for smoking awareness. We are looking forward to making presentations to local organizations and have been invited to present our program in Fall 2000 at the Safe and Drug Free Coordinators Conference. Our last goal is to design an evaluation tool so that we will know if the Living Textbook really helps people stop smoking. We have thought about using surveys, opinion polls, and feedback forms to give us some indication of the success of our project.

Software, Web Sites, and Other Resources Used for SWATS (Students Working Against Teen Smoking)

- Microsoft Word, PowerPoint, clip art CDs, Youth 97 CD, and Microsoft Publisher

- Digital cameras, CD burner, and scanner

- Pamphlets from the Centers for Disease Control, the American Lung Association, and the American Cancer Society

Helpful Hints

1. Secure parent volunteers to assist students with simulated digital pictures involving tobacco products.

2. Develop a parent release form for any student participating in the project.

3. Write minigrants for materials (e.g., digital camera, glossy paper, binders, CD-ROMs, etc.).

4. Contact your local substance abuse agency for materials, funding, support, and so forth.

5. Make sure that your English department has students write dialogue stories. Many of my students had never written a dialogue story, and they struggled with that part of the project.

6. Develop a weighted rubric for grading the presentations.

7. MAKE SURE THAT YOU HAVE A MEANS OF SAVING THE PROJECTS DIGITALLY. When the graphics are inserted, most of the PowerPoint presentations will not fit on a floppy disk. Make sure that your students have access to a common folder on a network drive or have access to a zip drive.

Conclusion

This project renewed my faith in today's teens. I have been teaching for 20 years, and it is so easy to think of teens as unmotivated and self-centered. In the Living Textbook project, I saw teens get involved because they truly cared about stopping other teens from smoking. As they created the dialogue stories, they really got involved with the issues that teens face with peer pressure to "fit in." Many of them continued working on their projects (on their own time) even when they knew that they had achieved an "A" on the project. They wanted their projects to be their best work. One group even surveyed students in the school, took their pictures, and scanned the images into their PowerPoint presentations. Another group created a collage from magazine articles and scanned the collage into their presentations. As a teacher, I watched my students take pride in their work, present in front of state representatives, and realize that they were making a difference in the lives of others.

▧ Keeping Rural South Dakota Students in Touch With the World

Brenda Lynch
Madison, South Dakota

I have long been an advocate for teachers creating their own Web sites in order for students to have a place to begin their research. What began for me as a very simple Web site has transformed into a place where students check grades, get extra help, research the library, listen to radio stations, read newspapers, download worksheets, and visit a variety of sites. From this repository of sites I have collected, I often get ideas that develop into what I think are culturally appropriate lessons, and these are important links for students in rural South Dakota. If you are curious to see this site, check http:/mhs.madison.k12.sd.us/lynchb/spanish/newsdpg.htm.

Here are some possible ideas of content to include on your Web site:

- Course descriptions

- Syllabus

- Supplies needed for the course

- Student grades (only by ID number)

- Grade scale

- Grading criteria you use

- Useful Web sites for your content area

- Assignments

- Lesson plans

- E-mail link to you

- Your teaching schedule and the best time to contact you

- Link to the school library

- PowerPoint presentations

- Cocurricular activities

- Committee information

- Photos (scanned or digital)

- Links to textbook companies (lesson plans and extra materials)

- Clip art Web sites

- Search engines (there are hundreds of these; find a couple that you like)

- Online dictionaries at http://www.facstaff.bucknell.edu/rbeard/diction.html

- Online calculators—many mortgage and car companies will figure interest and payments, or see http://www.ibeweb.org/IBE2/tools/calc/calculat.htm

- Banners that announce information (end of trimester, conferences, deadlines, etc.)

- Extra-credit work

- Personal information you want to share on the Web

- Your resumé

- Discussion boards (these are like open e-mail, where everyone can read what you wrote; this probably needs to be monitored closely)

- Counter (tells you how many visitors you have had)

- Newspapers, magazines, literature, organizations of interest to you

You may have seen other things that you like, so feel free to add to the list!!

Spanish Menu and Restaurant Project

A lesson that I have seen evolve the most with the use of technology is my food and menu unit. Every Spanish teacher probably needs to teach food at some point. After studying the vocabulary for different ingredients, we begin a cultural study of manners, recipes, currency, and eating in a restaurant. What has increased the value of the lesson for my students is the ability to research on the Internet.

They can research the country right along with the recipe and its ingredients. Internet recipes are usually more visually appealing than a black-and-white cookbook. I created a Web site for them that includes the lesson, recipes from different Spanish-speaking countries, table manners, and how to cook basic foods from Latin America (rice, tortillas, salsas, etc.).

The grammatical elements in this lesson include preterit verbs, food vocabulary, indirect and direct objects, and question words. Cultural elements include how various foods are eaten and prepared, table manners, currency exchange, and geographical review. If I were simply to teach the vocabulary and chapter for food, it would take three to four days; the chapter on preterit verbs, two to three days; on indirect objects, two to three days; on question words, one day; and on cultural manners and money exchange, one day. In total this lesson takes 10 days to complete, but I believe that doing it this way gives coherence to the curriculum and also places a real-life element in the classroom.

The lesson plan follows. Note that you can put your vocabulary criteria, grading criteria, and deadlines on your Web site.

Menu

To begin, use Web site: http://mhs.madison.k12.sd.us/lynchb/ spanish/ recipes.htm. You will be researching and writing a menu for a designated Spanish-speaking country. Your menu must include the following categories:

Aperitivos

Sopas

Verduras

Aves

Carnes

Mariscos

Ensaladas

Postres

Bebidas

Keep in mind the following requirements:

- Each category must have a minimum of two selections (except bebidas, which should include at least five authentic choices).

- The selections will be based on recipes that you found for your country.

- They must be culturally appropriate (i.e., no hamburguesas, pizzas, perros calientes!!!).

- For each item on the menu, you will write a description of the product (complete sentence). You do not need to describe the bebidas. This description may include the way it is made (grilled, fried, etc.), ingredients, or tastes (salada, rica, dulce, etc.). For example, "Pollo con salsa verde. ¡Servimos este plato

con pedazos grandes de pollo y una salsa muy rica!" "Fruta
fresca. ¡La mescla incluye sandias, melocotones, uvas, mangos
y un poquito azucar!"

■ The prices on your menu will be in the currency of your country.
   Your menu should be neat and attractive. Be sure to check spelling, sentence structure, and cultural appropriateness.

Restaurant Skit

Your group will be writing a script for a restaurant scene that will
include the following criteria:

You must use your menu and 40 food words.

You must use five place-setting words.

You must use five direct objects.

Props are to be used.

Pronunciation will be graded.

Your skit must be culturally appropriate.

Include a minimum of 15 lines per person that the class can understand.

Relationships in the Spanish-Speaking World: Spanish 4

Another example of practices that incorporate culture and advanced grammar can be seen in this lesson on relationships in the
Spanish-speaking world.

Big Ideas

Relationships

Dating and marriage in the Spanish-speaking world

Learner Outcomes

1. Students compare the customs of dating and marriage to U.S. customs.

2. Students communicate (in Spanish) with students in Spanish-speaking countries.

3. Students discuss their opinions of dating and marriage to compare them with what they have learned about others.

Evidence That Students Have Reached the Outcome

1. Students participate in an online project and use the Internet to research customs. Criteria include printed e-mail from partner school and cited Web sites.

2. Students create and present an authentic wedding scene based on their findings. Criteria include religious beliefs, family, legalities, and perspectives. They use video as the format of presentation.

Knowledge Needed

1. Future tense verbs

2. Subjunctive verbs

Skills Needed

1. Access e-mail and Internet

2. Discuss subjects of dating and marriage maturely

3. Use video appropriately

Teaching and Learning Experiences

Day 1

Brainstorm words and concepts regarding dating and marriage. Define vocabulary and explain project (see Day 4).

Day 2

Culture Standard 2.1—Cultural understanding of relationship between practices and perspectives: Go to computer lab to research customs and contact schools in the Spanish-speaking world (e-pals.com).

Day 3

Comparison Standard 4.2—Concept of culture through comparisons of the cultures studied and their own: Compare customs to our own in order to plan a wedding in which one person uses U.S. customs and the other person uses customs from a Spanish-speaking person.

Day 4

Communication Standard 1.2—Understand and interpret written and spoken language on a variety of topics:

- Work on writing skit.

- E-mail partner school with questions.

Day 5

Connections Standard 3.2—Acquire information and recognize the distinctive viewpoints that are only available through the foreign language and its culture:

- Review WEDDING (acronym for conditions of using subjunctive verbs).

- Incorporate sentences using the subjunctive into skits.

Day 6

Finish writing skits.

Day 7

Communication Standard 1.3—Present information, concepts, and ideas to an audience of listeners or readers on a variety of topics: Watch skits and answer questions about other groups' skits.

Student-Created Videos in the Spanish Classroom

I also love to use student-created video in my classroom. Here are some ideas students have developed to reinforce future tense verbs as well as my criteria and rules for using video created by students.

Ideas for a Video Set in the Future Tense

- Tell the story of your 30th class reunion.

- Describe what your life will be like 30 years from now.

- Tell what household appliances will be able to do in the year 2030.

- Imagine that you return to Madison High School 30 years from now. What will the school be like?

- Invent an imaginary world of the future.

- Describe Madison, South Dakota, in the future.

- What will children do for fun in the future?

- Give a newscast in the year 2030.

Other topics can be done with my permission. Note the following requirements:

- All skits must include 20 lines per person.

- Skits must include 20 future tense verbs.

- The action of the video must correspond to the script.

Video Reminders

1. I must be able to hear you on tape, or you will not get credit.

2. Use vocabulary that the class can understand. If you use a word unfamiliar to the class, find a way to demonstrate that in the video.

3. Be respectful while filming in the community. Ask permission to be in businesses.

4. Coordinate your schedules early. Not completing the video on time will affect your grade.

5. Remember my rules—Use your imagination to create something positive! NO SEX, NO DRUGS, NO ALCOHOL, NO VIOLENCE, and NO SWEARING.

Grading will be based on the following:

■ Written work—spelling, grammar, verb conjugations

■ Pronunciation and expression

■ Video production—use of class time, demonstration of the written action, and quality of the video (well edited, no driving around or unnecessary scenes, etc.)

Standards for this activity include the following:

Communication Standard 1.2—Students understand and interpret written and spoken language on a variety of topics.

Comparison Standard 4.1—Students demonstrate understanding of the nature of language through comparisons of the language studied to their own.

Communities Standard 5.1—Students use the language both within and beyond the school setting.

CHAPTER 6

Considering Special Needs

T his chapter looks at some successful programs that consider special needs.

🏴 Chapter Overview

■ **Rebecca Kelly,** a special education and inclusion teacher at Delmar Middle and High Schools in Delmar, Delaware, likes to use technology to build bridges between the students with disabilities and those without.

■ **Nancy Barnett,** the coordinator and author of the I CAN Work Program at Southside High School in Muncie, Indiana, explains how the I CAN Work Program is designed to service all areas of students with special needs.

▨ Integrating Inclusion in the Classroom With the Help of Technology

Rebecca Kelly
Delmar, Delaware

I am a special education teacher working in inclusion classrooms at the middle and high school levels. A large part of my job is to know my students' needs and to make the curriculum accessible to them. The inclusion classroom enables my students, who have mild to moderate disabilities, to experience the same opportunities as their nondisabled peers. With the growing importance of state standards and accountability, I believe they can achieve with the proper supports built into classroom activities. Teamwork and technology help make this achievement possible.

Inclusion is a difficult setting, which depends on a regular education teacher and a special education teacher combining talents to reach all of the students in the room. I check with the regular education teachers on a regular basis regarding the scope and sequence of their lessons and how certain modifications can be made to meet the Individual Education Plan (IEP) goals set for certain students.

Also taken into consideration is the incorporation of state standards, which affect all students who plan to graduate with a diploma. The teamwork of the two teachers can make or break an inclusion classroom. The special education teacher may feel like an outsider coming into someone else's classroom; similarly, the regular education teacher may feel that the other teacher is intruding into his or her territory. To quell these feelings, it is often helpful for both parties to agree on the roles they will take within the classroom before the school year starts.

The two teachers must agree on which model suits them best: team teaching, where they coteach simultaneously; leader/support team, where the regular education teacher gives the direct instruction and the special education teacher conducts the reteaching section of the lesson; or the visible/invisible team, where the regular education teacher handles the direct instruction, and the special education teacher modifies tests and assignments, handles the grading, and works one on one with students when necessary.

It is important that both teachers agree to discipline rules, classroom procedures, and grading scales prior to the start of the school year; otherwise, the students will try to play one teacher against the other. If it is the first year for either teacher, I would recommend a simple contract outlining which duties will be handled by one teacher or shared by both. This will help set initial parameters in the room and also help explain your working relationship if one or both of you happen to be observed by an administrator or parent during the inclusion class time.

With the teamwork in place, I then proceed to suggest ways to include all the students in the room. Cooperative lessons help accomplish this goal. Even at the high school level, individual strengths tend to surface when shared within a mixed group. Never make up a group of "the lowest kids"; this approach isn't fair to them or to anyone else in the group. All students need to be challenged so that they can have an opportunity to shine. A student who is weak in reading and writing might be an outstanding group speaker. Likewise, the shy one in the group may be the best organizer of information.

I like to use technology to build bridges between the students with disabilities and those without. Because I didn't have a computer to use, I wrote a grant proposal to Americorps and received recycled computers capable of connecting to the Internet and carrying the basic programs—Microsoft Word, Microsoft PowerPoint, and Netscape Composer—that I needed. With limited funds, I was able to procure the hardware and software I needed; some of the applications could be downloaded for free from the Internet. As a result, I was able to institute two specific methods: cooperative PowerPoint presentations and class-created WebQuests.

Cooperative PowerPoint presentations can provide enrichment of a particular concept, remediation of a skill, or conclusion of a specific unit. All you need to get started is a computer, Microsoft PowerPoint (which can be found in Microsoft Office), and some method to present it to the class. Presentation options can be as simple as printing out the slides and copying them onto overhead transparencies or as complex as using an LCD panel or multimedia projector. To incorporate a cooperative PowerPoint presentation, you need to follow four basic steps:

1. *Preparation*—Take time to work with the PowerPoint program and find out what its capabilities are. Decide what length the class's presentation will be (a presentation of 12 slides will fill up a 40-minute time slot). Decide which elements (i.e., graphics, photographs, etc.) will be used. When a set number of slides has been decided, create a blank PowerPoint presentation with that selected number of slides. This approach will come in handy in Step 2. As always, SAVE EVERYTHING along the way. You never know when the power will go off or the fire drill bell will sound.

2. *Brainstorming/Slide creation*—Use a story board to outline the class presentation. If the class is going to create a presentation with 12 slides, then identify the topic or focus of each of those slides and assign them to small groups of two to three students. Students will then create a draft of the information they plan to put on the slide, complete with any artwork or clip art they plan to include. Once their drafts have been approved, use the slide sorter function on the PowerPoint presentation previously saved and click on the number of their slide. At this point, they will insert the information on the computer screen and save it.

3. *Prepresentation*—At this time, teacher editing comes into play to double-check spelling and grammar. Make sure all equipment is hooked up and operating properly prior to the class period in which the students will be giving the presentation. It is advisable to make a backup copy of the presentation on the hard drive as well as on a floppy disk or zip disk just to

be safe. Print out handouts, such as the outline view, to help keep other students focused on the lesson.

4. *Showtime!*—As each slide of the presentation is shown, have each small group get up and explain its slide. Because of space constraints, a slide can only hold main ideas, which affords students the opportunity to elaborate on those main ideas without having to write it down. If this approach is used as a review for a final test on a unit, encourage discussion and note taking.

Delaware English/language arts standards that are met by this approach include the following:

■ Students use written and oral English appropriate for various purposes and audiences.

■ Students construct, examine, and extend the meaning of literary, informative, and technical texts through listening, reading, and viewing.

■ Students gain access, organize, and evaluate information gained by listening, reading, and viewing.

Another approach that works well in the inclusion classroom is the use of WebQuests. This approach focuses on how a Web-based lesson design can accommodate a variety of disabilities within the regular education classroom. A six-component model, originated by Bernie Dodge, guides teachers and students through the inquiry-based lesson. I created a checklist and planner to help teachers and students create a WebQuest, with step-by-step instructions on how to implement this design in the inclusion classroom.

The lesson then provides guided research using the Internet while incorporating a variety of skills including problem solving. This particular practice received the 1999 Project IDEA (Identifying and Disseminating Educational Alternatives) award from the Delaware

Department of Education and the Exceptional Children and Early Childhood Group.

The WebQuest is especially helpful for meeting the needs of students with disabilities within the general education classroom. Students with special needs sometimes suffer from information overload when first learning about computer programs; consequently, they need lists of steps to follow. Instructional support can be incorporated into the design of the WebQuest in the form of readability, larger text, and simpler directions. Also, because schools and teachers are required to help the child be involved in and progress within the general education curriculum, the WebQuest format offers the opportunity to incorporate basic skills with higher-order thinking skills and other enrichment activities with other nondisabled peers.

The first step in designing a WebQuest is creating a draft of the Web page. This can be accomplished by the teacher alone or with the input of the students. The initial information necessary—the classroom objectives, IEP objectives, and state standards—should be identified at the initiation of the WebQuest.

One example is "SOS—Salvaging One Sunken Ship," a WebQuest created in coordination with my eighth-grade students' American History, English, and Reading classes (http://www.k12.de.us/delmar/school/projects/webquest/sos/sos.html). About half of the students in this class of 22 had reading and written expression goals on their IEPs, with documented levels ranging from second grade to sixth grade. This group also included students identified with disabilities in the areas of expressive and receptive language, learning disabilities, hearing impairments, and educably mentally handicapped. Fostering teamwork and cooperative learning are also important goals while still providing modifications as stated in the student IEPs. The teamwork is modeled for the students by the coordination between the general education teacher and the special education teacher.

In the case of the SOS WebQuest, I solicited the help of the reading specialist in the creation stage of the lesson. The specialist assisted with a relevant historical fiction book at a lower reading level and several Internet links regarding shipwrecks and the International Ice Patrol that she had collected over the past few years. With her material and my background in educational technology and special education, we proceeded forward with our integrated WebQuest. The six components of a WebQuest are Introduction, Task, Resources, Process, Evaluation, and Conclusion:

1. The introduction provides an overview and essential background information of the lesson.

2. The task can also be referred to as the problem, because it states the student's role in solving a specific problem or situation.

3. Resources consist of the Internet links, which are preselected.

4. The process consists of steps that guide the students toward reaching their goal. (Simplifying language to accommodate low reading ability is very easy to incorporate in this stage. The steps can be broken down into as many as needed for the student to be successful.)

5. Evaluation tells students how they will be graded on completion of the lesson.

6. The conclusion states cross-curricular objectives that the student has successfully accomplished with the completion of the activity.

If a page editor is not available to create Web pages, do not fear. Netscape Communicator has a component called Netscape Composer, a user-friendly page editor, that is downloadable and available at no cost. Using the page editor, creation of the WebQuest begins with headings, text, and even pictures. With a few simple steps, a URL address becomes an active link to the Internet.

Once the page has been created in an HTML format, the teacher has two choices. First, the page can be placed into a folder on the computer, saved to a disk, and then uploaded via the school's server.

The second choice involves saving the document to a classroom computer's hard drive. The links will still work the same, but in the second case, that specific computer is the only machine that can access the file. The integrated unit usually takes about four to five class periods (about 50 minutes each) to complete. The first period should be used as an overview of the contents and usage of the WebQuest, with the next two to three sessions involved in searching the Web sites linked to the WebQuest page. The final period or two can be spent working on the solution or problem-solving activity noted in the Task part of the lesson. An example of this lesson can be found at "SOS: Salvaging One Sunken Ship" (http://www.k12.de.us/delmar/school/projects/webquest/sos/sos.html). More information on WebQuests is located at "The WebQuest Page" (http://edweb.sdsu.edu/webquest/webquest.html).

Technologies to Help Accommodate Special Needs

If a special needs student needs additional assistance in the inclusion classroom, I have found the following technologies helpful:

1. If the student is strong orally but weak in writing, try a word-recognition program such as Via Voice.

2. If a student needs help with the correction of spelling and punctuation skills, a mini-word processor such as NTS Dreamwriter ($250) or a software program such as Microsoft Word will show misspelled words and offer spell-check options. Franklin spellers are another way to approach this problem.

3. If a student has difficulty remembering the equation he or she put into a regular calculator, try a graphing calculator; it will show the entire equation and the answer so the student can check the input and result of the work to find his or her own errors.

4. If a student has low vision or needs auditory and visual input simultaneously because of poor visual memory skills, try a

screen reader such as Kurzweil 3000. This program is more expensive, but it enables a teacher to put any text (book, test, etc.) on a scanner, and the program will read it aloud to the student while highlighting it on the screen.

Helpful Tips

1. Build a teamwork approach within the inclusion classroom. It is as important for the teachers to model how to work together as it is for the students.

2. Explore new uses for familiar applications. Spreadsheet applications can help students graph and chart data without having to buy new software.

3. Write grants. To date, I have received over $6,000 in equipment and software by simply putting my ideas on paper. Be specific about your needs and how your idea will benefit the learning outcomes of all of your students.

4. Know your students. Build on their strengths. Never assume they can't do something; that's the time they will always surprise you. Remember, taking small steps still denotes forward movement.

The I CAN Work Program

Nancy Barnett
Muncie, Indiana

The I CAN Work Program is designed to serve all types of students with special needs by helping them to improve themselves by working in their own business, producing and selling products they help design. Using a service learning teaching model, the students take part in every facet of the business, with each student matched to those areas in which he or she can best develop. Through their participation, students improve their self-esteem and personal skills. They project a positive image to the community, showing what special needs kids are capable of accomplishing, while eventually creating opportunities for regular education students to join them in their enterprise.

I CAN works to build self-esteem in individuals through various means. Students develop pride in quality workmanship, work completion, and retail sales, and they gain acceptance and respect from their community. Those who are able become peer supervisors, and all learn skills that will be applicable to other jobs, home life, and community participation.

Special needs students staff as many jobs as possible: cutting, assembly, woodworking, packaging, mailing, labeling, cleaning, painting, shop sales, and inspection, for example. Remaining jobs that need additional supervision, such as making bank deposits, are staffed with job coaches, parent volunteers, or Ball State University participants assisting the I CAN worker. In weekly group meetings, students and staff discuss products, work schedules, performance, and peer relationships. Jobs are rotated, and new responsibilities are discussed and demonstrated. Students learn to work with lower levels of prompting and assistance and less reliance on adults, therefore increasing their quality of life.

The I CAN project is unlike most sheltered workshops programs in that participants have control over their own product, their own jobs, and sales. In essence, they control their own business, a business they have helped build to accommodate themselves. The program actually is more similar to Junior Achievement in operation. As the program has grown, opportunities have been offered to regular education students and school faculty to display and sell their products in the I CAN store and catalog. Regular education students are encouraged to work with I CAN workers after school and during the student resource time period.

The service-learning teaching model of linking learning to meaningful service has enabled our special education students, who are traditionally on the receiving end of the giving of others, to give and grow. We are able to observe an improved attitude, better attendance, reduced discipline problems, and increased awareness of community needs from the I CAN participants.

These students have used the I CAN store profits to buy $500 worth of toys for the Toys for Tots Christmas program; to assemble baskets full of items for the home and present them to 26 new Habitat for Humanity homeowners; to make quilts for ABC Quilts, which are sent to AIDS babies; and to host a community luncheon for leaders in the community so they could observe our school working for the community in a positive way.

In the past five years, as the author of the I CAN Work Program, I have been privileged to share and assist other I CAN programs around the state. Presently, there are eight similar programs. During the school year, we are hosts to numerous teacher groups that visit I CAN wanting to start programs also. My goal is to continue with the present program and assist any new start-up programs. As a special needs teacher from Muncie, Indiana, I am anxious to share the I CAN Work Program with fellow teachers in Russia. Our school would be honored to exchange information with special educators and classes in Russia.

Parents of I CAN students have nothing but praise for the program their children participate in, but they end up asking "What is out there, similar to I CAN, for my child when he or she leaves high school?" Up to now, the answer has been "Very little other than sheltered workshops." However, we are developing plans for a BEYOND I CAN Program for this post-high school population. It will be a program in cooperation with the State of Indiana and a carryover from I CAN to create a manufacturing business that will employ special needs clients (51%) and the regular population (49%); it will be called an "affirmative industry."

Clients will work together on state contracts and will produce a card line that will be marketed to nonprofit organizations to use as fund-raisers. Plans call for the continuation of service learning in the program, meaning that a portion of the profits will be used for community projects voted on by the clients. It is not expected that every client will work a 40-hour week; therefore, a community volunteer component will be included in which clients receive training on how to give back to their community through volunteerism.

CHAPTER 7

Teaching Social Studies and Geography in the High School Grades

This chapter offers award-winning ways to teach social studies and geography in the high school grades.

🖹 Chapter Overview

- ■ **James Wade D'Acosta**, a social studies teacher at Fairfield High School in Fairfield, Connecticut, assigns students "reading projects."

- ■ **Janine A. Jellander,** a secondary social science teacher at Mira Costa High School in Manhattan Beach, California, says that "one way to ensure quality instruction and promote intrinsic motivation is to integrate various curricula with the core subject matter as well as to involve integration strategies with other subject areas."

■ **James Wade D'Acosta,** a social studies teacher at Fairfield High School in Fairfield, Connecticut, uses scenario groups. He says that "creating first-person accounts from different points of view stretches the creativity and problem-solving abilities of students."

Reading Books Instead of Book Reviews

James Wade D'Acosta
Fairfield, Connecticut

Q. Why do students lie about reading books?

A. Because teachers choose the books.

Q. Why do students choose short books when given a choice?

A. Because teachers ask them to read "a book," regardless of length.

Q. Why do students plagiarize from professional book reviews when writing papers about books?

A. Because teachers ask students to summarize books and analyze plots.

GOALS

1. To encourage students to read

2. To give students a positive experience reading adult fiction and nonfiction books related to the course in order to encourage them to do so in the years ahead

3. To demonstrate to students how writing can enrich their understanding of books they read

SOLUTIONS

Through my own guilty experience as a student, I realized that students have good reasons for not reading assigned books and for plagiarizing professional book reviews in their writing. I didn't have time to read everything I was assigned, and much of it didn't interest me anyway. I wasn't allowed to write about aspects of books that made them interesting to me personally.

As a teacher of American History, Highlights of Western Civilization, Politics, and Economics, I give students as broad a range as possible in choosing books to read. I call these "reading projects" and assign 20% of the marking period grade as both motivation and reward for the time and effort I'm requiring. In American History, during the second marking period, for example, I accept fiction and nonfiction books written on any topic in American history or any book written by an American author who lived between 1840 and 1890.

Therefore, students choose topics as varied as the California Gold Rush, the Mexican War, the Civil War, the last Indian wars, Western expansion, and industrial development. Books on these topics include biographies, journals, historical fiction such as Michael Shaara's *Killer Angels,* Louisa May Alcott's *Little Women,* and Alex Haley's *Roots.* Students may read books by Mark Twain or a Twain biography. They may read collected stories of Ambrose Bierce or his biography. Furthermore, this flexibility lends itself to interdisciplinary connections between American history and American literature whether a formal American Studies course exists or not.

Once students have flexibility, I eliminate the temptation to read short books by asking for a certain number of hours, not for the completion of "a book." For example, for honors students I require 4 hours each week for four weeks. Thus, a total of 16 hours brings students into "B" range (I reserve "A" grades for quality and effort that are "above and beyond," say 20 hours or more).

If a slow reader chooses *Roots* but does not finish after reading for 20 hours, no problem—he is still in the running for an "A," depending on the quality of his writing. If a fast reader chooses *Little Women* and finishes in 8 hours, she must continue to read. Options include other books by Alcott, a biography of Alcott, or another book with a Civil War setting.

The playing field for grades is leveled among all students. The fast readers and the slow readers must put in the same amount of time. If fast readers complain, I say "Your reward is more knowledge. " If slow readers reveal dyslexia, I say "No problem, I'm not looking for speed; read every page four times if you have to." Course evaluations written by students over the past 10 years confirm that students do in fact do the reading, although many admit to some degree of fabrication in the number of hours they claim. I don't win every battle.

The majority of the writing I require with this "reading project" is in the form of a personal, "dialectical" journal. I subscribe to the theory that each individual reader creates his or her own meaning when confronted with a text. We each have different perspectives and backgrounds. The meaning of a book is created during the interaction between the author's words and the reader's reaction.

In the extreme, this position maintains that a book never has exactly the same meaning even when read by the same person over and over again. Simply put, what makes a book enjoyable and meaningful varies from person to person and is not usually related to an analysis or summary of the plot.

I enjoy reading about the American Civil War, a.k.a. "The War Between the States," a.k.a. "The War of Northern Aggression," because my ancestors fought against each other and because I've lived in both northern and southern states. When I read a book about the war, I get excited at the mention of people and places that relate to my family's experience. These are usually along the periphery of the main action in the book, but they are the reason I'm reading the book. I *want* to think about these seemingly minor people and places. I *need* to express myself about these people and places. My mind is focused on them, and if I'm asked to write about what I think, it is a pleasure and a release. If I am asked merely to summarize and analyze the plot, I'll go to a professional book review to make sure I get it right and to maintain my high grade point average.

In a personal, dialectical journal, students react to specific passages that they choose. They quote the passage and then write a personal but not private reaction. Perhaps they like or dislike the passage. Maybe they don't understand what's going on or need to look up a historical reference. They may be able to relate to the action because of a similar personal experience.

In my assignment, they must write 2 such pages each week over the course of four weeks, for a total of 8 pages, for consideration for a "B," depending on the depth and quality of their writing. Again, for an "A" they must go above and beyond, say 10 or 12 quality pages. Sometimes they have much to write, sometimes not. I look for thoughtfulness and for a variety of types of reactions: some memories, some considerations of right or wrong, some looking up of words.

The assignment ends with a polished, 4-page typed paper in which students explain what they read, why they chose the topic, and how it affected them. I analyze the way they condense and deepen their personal reactions from their journals. They may earn extra credit by producing a poster to share with the class or by watching a movie or documentary related to what they've read.

National Standards

This assignment meets Standards II and IX of the National Early Adolescence/Social Studies-History Standards. Standard II is "Valuing Diversity: Accomplished teachers understand that each student brings diverse perspectives to any experience." The emphasis on personal journal writing places high value on each student's unique perspective. Standard IX is "Assessment: Accomplished teachers employ a variety of assessment methods." Asking students to read for a certain amount of time and combining the fulfillment of this requirement with first-draft journal writing and a short polished paper creates variety and creativity in the assessment of the final product.

Helpful Tips

1. Bring in books you've recently read yourself. Display your enthusiasm—it's infectious. Students need to see that adults read.

2. Do not limit students to a list of books you've read. Give them as much freedom as possible.

3. Keep a list of the books students choose. This not only gives you more books to suggest the following year but also provides you with excellent insight into issues that concern each unique group and generation of students. I got turned on to Malcolm X by an eighth-grade student two years before Spike Lee's movie. His journal was fascinating. I read *The Autobiography of Malcolm X* the following summer and was prepared for the explosive interest among students once the movie came out.

4. Get help. I'm not an English teacher. I was introduced to reading and writing theories and to dialectical journals by the Connecticut Writing Project. National Writing Project members sponsor workshops everywhere. Seek them out—they're a bright, motivated bunch with a lot to teach all of us.

▧ Teacher for a Day

Janine A. Jellander
Manhattan Beach, California

Making learning meaningful is fundamental to student motivation. One way to ensure quality instruction and promote intrinsic motivation is to integrate various curricula with the core subject matter as well as to involve integration strategies with other subject areas.

Geography is an especially well-suited integrative study in the field of the social sciences.

National and international events of the past decade have led to an increasing awareness of the need to improve geographic literacy in the United States. Although geography is not a mandated course in most states, national geography standards have been written to encourage and challenge students to become geographically aware. A global perspective enables students to ask and answer geographic questions, analyze and solve problems, evaluate consequences of different courses of action, and learn to embrace and accept diversity.

It is well established that assessing student knowledge and achievement involves evaluating higher-level thinking—including analysis, synthesis, and evaluation—through performance-based assessment. Although this type of assessment may be both time consuming and more subjective in evaluation, it does allow the quality of the instrument to depend mainly on the skill of the student rather than on the skill of the test constructor.

The purpose of the following activity is to encourage students to investigate, analyze, and discuss how people depend upon, adapt to, are affected by, and change the natural environment. This project gives students the opportunity to demonstrate how they can apply and use their learning in solving problems and making decisions. Furthermore, this assignment introduces students to speaking in front of their peers in the role of the teacher rather than the student. As a culmination to a unit or course in geography and global issues, students are placed in team-teaching pairs to present a global topic of their choice. This project is divided into three components: lesson plan preparation, lesson presentation, and an individual research statement based on the lesson topic.

As an introduction to the project, students may be asked to write an evaluative essay based on a teacher-created prompt. This essay should focus on the factors that students deem necessary in the classroom to promote learning. The goal of this motivational activity is to encourage students to identify and analyze the strategies that they could use in their presentations. This assignment also serves as a tool for the teacher to better understand his or her instruction from a student perspective and to evaluate his or her pedagogical strategies to meet individual student needs.

Another prelude to the project could be the examination of a professional development video for practicing teachers on best classroom practices and strategies. It is anticipated that students will be engaged by the methods demonstrated to solicit student participation and retention of information. This focus activity also serves to illustrate the rigor and professionalism of the teaching vocation.

It is critical that students learn the importance of preparation in presentation design and execution. Students are introduced to a sample lesson plan that is designed to demonstrate how the various components of a lesson can be used. Although lesson plans are written for different grade levels and subject areas, the lesson type can be used for all students, regardless of age, ability, or content area.

The teacher should explain and model a traditional seven-step lesson plan that includes an objective, motivational activity, materials, development, methods, closing, and home learning. Students should also be familiarized with the importance of time management for the lesson presentation.

Next, students are encouraged to select a topic that will maintain student curiosity and involvement. Students are expected to become "experts" on the selected topic through scholastic research. Students are encouraged to use a variety of resources to develop a wealth of material for their presentations. Practice or review of accessing library resources, multimedia, and the Internet may be necessary to develop the research process. Whereas the lesson plan and presentation are assessed collaboratively, students are held individually accountable for the development and submission of an essay providing a description and the significance of their selected topics.

The final component to the project involves teaching to the class. To better prepare students in the areas of time management and presentation design and delivery, be sure to identify the time constraints and exhibition skills necessary for effective lesson presentations. Encourage the team-teaching partners to use creativity in their lesson designs. For example, teaching partners may choose to use activity-based or cooperative learning strategies versus a traditional teacher-directed teaching model in their presentation.

This activity is extremely motivating because it challenges students to maintain the interest of their peers, overcome fears of public speaking, and introduce them to a potential career in the teaching profession.

Performance-based assessment should be meaningful to both the student and the teacher. The teacher and student should understand the standards and criteria for assessment in advance so that students may plan and organize their work accordingly. As the primary evaluator of the presentations, the teacher must devise and share with students a rubric that students can actively use to plan and assess their own performance. Furthermore, the recent trend in peer assistance review in the teaching profession may also be applicable to the student presentations. It is recommended that students videotape and critically analyze each other's lessons. If impeded by time constraints, ask team teachers to write a reflective essay on their own performance highlighting effective pedagogical practices and areas of improvement.

Helpful Tips

1. *Integrate student presentations.* Based on the student-selected topics, create a calendar of presentations throughout the year (or semester) that coincide with your unit design. Students will recognize the significance of their lesson as they act as guest teachers for a day.

2. *Emphasize the weight of the activity.* It is a fun project but one that requires a lot of hard work, time management, and creativity.

3. *Establish professionalism.* Be sure to establish a professional tone and environment during each presentation. Establish classroom rules for guest speakers and follow through with consequences for poor behavior.

4. *Encourage student creativity and autonomy.* Be supportive of new ideas, and guide students. Acting as their mentor rather than their evaluator will help encourage students to expand their ideas beyond those previously demonstrated by you.

5. *Seek parent support.* Given the nature and weight of the assignment, require all students and parents to sign an assignment contract. This contract serves to keep parents informed and involved in their child's learning.

6. *Evaluate the project.* Ask students to assess the effectiveness of the presentations. Together, determine and address the areas of improvement for future inclusion of the project in your classroom.

Scenario Groups

James Wade D'Acosta
Fairfield, Connecticut

CHALLENGES

1. How to get students to understand that people in the past were not simply good, bad, or stupid

2. How to get students to use historical documents and primary sources and live to say the experience was fun

SOLUTION

Put students into scenario groups and have them write historical fiction.

A scenario group is a small group of students, say three, who pretend to occupy the same historical time, place, and situation. Each student faces the situation from a different point of view. For example, the place may be Nottoway Plantation on the Mississippi River in Louisiana. One student pretends to be a member of the master's family, another is a slave, and the third is a visitor from Connecticut. Each student produces two or more fictional letters or diary entries based on research materials provided by the teacher: tourist brochures of Nottoway or access to books or Internet sites with images of the plantation, copies of newspapers from the period containing advertisements for runaway slaves and slave auctions, and slave narratives such as that of Frederick Douglass.

Students help each other gather historically verifiable and believable facts, but they must remain in character in their individual writing assignments. Staying in character forces each member of the group to recognize the complexity of the historical situation: Slave masters were motivated by concern for the economic well-being of their family, peer pressure from their neighbors, safety, and habit when confronted with the question of continuing to use slave labor. Slaves considered separation from their family and friends; not knowing where to go, how to get there, or what they'd do once they escaped; and severe penalties if captured. Visitors were restrained by manners, peer pressure, and severe penalties if they even considered helping a slave escape.

Assessment is ongoing and individual. The teacher measures each student's learning by noting diligence in gathering information, the level of cooperation within each group, and the quality of each student's individual research and written work. A large part of what makes this assignment fun is the freedom afforded by historical fiction. The plot is up to the students. They may create an elaborate escape. Writing about the motivation and mechanics can be a blast.

A historically verifiable fact can be as simple as having a character jump off the second-floor balcony of the plantation home at

Nottoway, verified by the fact that photographs of the home in tourist brochures show a second-story balcony. A slave bludgeoning an owner with a silver candlestick in the dining room, someone picking up a particular piece of furniture, or someone running down the hall in a specific direction to get outside—all these contain factual elements derived from the layout of the house.

One of the beauties of this assignment is that the scenario group can be placed anywhere and at any time in history as long as the teacher can provide enough sources for students to use in gathering facts. Tourist brochures are very effective and hold the additional promise of inspiring students to actually visit in the years ahead. Brochures, tourist books, and Internet sites are available for many museums around the world.

Creating first-person accounts from different points of view stretches the creativity and problem-solving abilities of students. Scenario grouping also creates a virtual field trip, an intimate experience for each student with any place, circumstance, and period in history. Imagination grounded in historical fact is akin to time travel. It's the next best thing to being there. Students recognize that people in the past were as well intentioned, complex, and human as themselves.

National Standards

This assignment fulfills Standard IV of the National Early Adolescence/Social Studies-History Standards. Standard IV is "Advancing Disciplinary Knowledge and Understanding: Accomplished teachers have a repertoire of strategies and techniques that engage student interest in and advance student understanding of United States History, World History, Economics, Political Science, and Geography." Scenario grouping grounded in historical facts forces students to consider a wide range of factors that contribute to ways of life and decisions people make given certain circumstances.

Helpful Tips

Students respond well to holding tourist brochures in their hands. Historic places are run by friendly people who love history. The use and circulation of these brochures is good advertising. Pick up several copies of their brochures when you visit during vacations or business trips. The next best thing to a tourist brochure is an Internet site. Many historic places have their own virtual guided tours up on the Web.

CHAPTER 8

Looking at Visual Arts and Physical Education

T his chapter looks at visual arts and physical education in a new millennium.

Chapter Overview

■ **Diana W. McDougal,** an art educator at Cheyenne East High School in Cheyenne, Wyoming, says her instructional strategy is "to develop a curriculum structure that will engage students in the course activity in a way that makes it almost impossible to be a passive participant."

■ **Nancy J. Pudas,** a physical education teacher at Eden Prairie High School in Eden Prairie, Minnesota, asks, "What makes a good physical education program these days?"

Visual Arts Standards and Creativity

Diana W. McDougal
Cheyenne, Wyoming

Matching the Visual Arts Standards with a course structured on the Creative Process is the best way to raise the level of student achievement.

After hours of collaborative effort to establish standards for visual arts in my district, Maslov's hierarchy kicked in, and basic survival instinct launched a best practice for me. I developed a personal guiding statement. I needed to clarify my own instructional direction, one based on what I believe to be the core components of an exemplary art program. My professional goal is to facilitate learning so that every one of my students becomes both an informed interpreter of art in many forms and also an independent creator of unique and original art.

In high school, students are given more choices. The visual art courses in our school are electives and are media specific (Drawing, Painting, Sculpture, etc.), not level sequential (Art I, II, III). This places students with no prior art experience in courses with students aspiring to earn scholarships for advancement into higher education and art careers.

Pre-International Baccalaureate freshmen and sophomore students are in classes with other sophomores, juniors, and seniors. Although they all elected the course, students still make strategic choices about how to use their time and invest their efforts. They choose a course and then decide whether to put forth effort or to slide by with a minimum.

Raising standards will probably not raise the motivation of students to sustain higher levels of achievement. In fact, students are aware that standards increased only by degree the quality and quantity of work needed to slide by with a minimum effort. Therefore, my instructional strategy has been to develop a curriculum structure that will engage students in the course activity in a way that makes it almost impossible to be a passive participant.

I teach Drawing, Acrylic/Oil Painting, and Art Computer Graphics. I begin all three of my courses with three mini-units. The first mini-unit is totally instructor guided. Subsequent units decrease in teacher-guided components and increase student initiative and accountability. Students are immediately engaged in a six-step *Creative Process.* The six steps are as follows:

1. *Clarify* by learning the vocabulary, by asking questions, and by defining the direction in concept, intent, purpose, and importance.

2. *Ideate* for originality by first inquiring or researching what has already been or is currently being done with the related fundamentals of art and then by using strategies that build fluency and flexibility in thinking

3. *Practice* both the process and technical media skills by creating composition plans or prototypes; experience and solve the technical and design problems.

4. *Create* a summation piece (final product) that demonstrates quality and that evidences complexity in the development of both technical skill and also depth of intellectual and conceptual thinking.

5. *Evaluate* by writing a comprehensive reflective statement on the Creative Process that includes a self-evaluation.

6. *Evidence personal connections* to other academic study, to life experience, or to a career.

The first mini-unit guides students through all six steps. In the second mini-unit, the teacher guides students through four of the six steps (1, 3, 4, and 6), and in the third, students are guided through two steps (1 and 3). In a fourth unit, students are guided only through Step 1, which seems to be the greatest challenge to students. With each mini-unit, students are given choices that compel them to be more self-directed. Subsequent projects are all student generated, and students may follow a serendipitous approach through the Creative Process; however, they are expected to write a statement of intent and conclude with a reflective summary. An oral presentation to the class is an optional substitution for the written reflective statement.

The mini-units are sequential to cover the three fundamentals of art and the three main categories of art styles. I present the fundamentals of art as (a) content (concept, intent, purpose, meaning, or importance of the art work or artifact); (b) form (the structure and materials of art, such as bronze sculpture, tonal pencil drawing, watercolor painting, etc.); and (c) technique (style—the categories of art—and method—technical skill and process). I define the categories of art as literal (based upon realism), expressive (based upon mood, emotion, feeling), and formal (based upon the elements and principles of design, or upon the rules of math and science, such as the use of formal perspective).

The summation piece (final product) does not receive the greatest weight in the assessment of each student. A portfolio, or body of work completed through the Creative Process, is assessed as a whole. Students are responsible for presenting a complete portfolio of the following:

1. Their sketchbook-workbook, which includes
   a. An organized, sequential demonstration of process with notes taken during demonstration; individual responses to vocabulary, terms, phrases, and names of key artists or art periods
   b. Evidence of research or inquiry in depth and breadth with a variety of selections from content, form, and technique of contemporary or master artists
   c. Technical and composition practices
   d. Independent student annotations during the process

2. A summation piece of exhibit quality

3. A final reflective statement that summarizes experience and evidences student connection to other disciplines or life experience

The emphasis in all units and projects is on originality in content (the concept, idea, purpose, importance, or meaning of the final piece) and on an imaginative approach or innovative inclusion of new technology during the practice step of the Creative Process.

All of the first mini-units begin with the formal technical category. Students are immediately engaged with a personal response to a concept or technique. For example, the first mini-unit in my Acrylic/Oil Painting course is a symbolic self-portrait. I try not to lecture or give clues for responses. I begin by handing out a blank simplified structure of the color wheel. Students are asked to quickly fill in the primary and secondary colors using the large color wheel hanging in the room as a reference. I then ask them to respond emotionally, physiologically, and intellectually to all six colors by making annotations near each color around the wheel. We then have a brief, nonthreatening sharing of responses. This opens a discussion on whether or not human response to color intellectually, emotionally, and physiologically is universal, crossing both time and distance.

Students naturally begin to categorize responses. Are they universal, or are they based upon a contemporary media or literary bias, as in "red badge of courage," "mellow yellow," "green with envy"? Can the other senses be involved? Can you taste or hear color? Discussion on scientific research concerning color and multiple color systems usually follows. I then introduce questions about color associations to nonobjective shapes. What color is a triangle? A square? A circle? Do geometric shapes evoke a different translation in color than organic shapes?

Students are then given direction to create a symbolic self-portrait using three colors. Questions about the parameters of three colors usually open the communication to identify the three contrasts of color (value, intensity, and temperature) and their variations, which include tints, shades, and neutrals. As students begin the ideation stage, they are encouraged to focus on two or three personality traits or moral or ethical codes that best identify their own character.

During the first five steps of the mini-unit, I bring in books on specific artists, including Wassily Kandinsky, Joan Miró, and Paul Klee. I also bring in a variety of books on color theory and articles and books on scientific research concerning the human response to color. Students are given time to "research" in class and to add bibliographical information and annotations to their sketchbook-workbooks.

In the class period following this first mini-unit deadline we hold a formal class critique. Students' reflective statements are taped to the backs of the paintings. I teach two sections of the same course, so I have each class critique the alternate class's work for anonymity. I ask students to respond as a group to each of the paintings, one at a time, as if they were meeting the artist. "If this person walked into the room, what would he or she be like? What can you tell about this person by his or her choice of color, shape, placement, and proportions of color? What was he or she trying to tell us by these choices?"

I allow enough time for adequate responses, and then I read only the paragraph of the reflective statement that identifies the student artist's intent. Students are amazed and excited as they discover that their individual and collective interpretations are astutely accurate. It is a very nonthreatening and fun way for students to learn to evaluate using specific criteria. Many students have told me later that this assignment helped them understand formal, nonobjective art.

I begin the second mini-unit with a demonstration on double- and triple-loading paint brushes. Students practice on heavy brown kraft paper and are asked to cut out and glue the best practice examples into their sketchbook-workbooks for reference. The focus of this unit is on the expressionistic category of art, and the minipainting is of a floral still life. Supplied references include European tole painting technique books, a Helen Van Wyk video on painting *Flowers Alla Prima,* and a variety of art books on Expressionists and Impressionists.

The third mini-unit is a black, white, and gray tonal under-painting. I use a variety of white basic forms in a still life. After the students complete a realistic, technically exact blended minipainting in the literal category, the paintings are varnished with gloss medium. I add three spotlights over the still life, with one each of a red, yellow, and blue lightbulb. Students then visually experience the phenomenon of the complementary color exchange that occurs on the objects and in the shadows. They are asked to translate what they see using the glazing technique over their varnished underpaintings.

By the time students complete all three projects, they have completed one each of formal, expressive, and literal categories. They have also had experience with a flat paint application, double- and triple-loading *alla prima* style, and underpainting with glazing. They have also been guided through the Creative Process three times and are ready for more choices in content and technique. All the state and national art standards have been applied, and the structure also supports language art standards.

My exams are not traditional vocabulary and multiple-choice exams. They are extended-response, take-home tests. I list on a sheet of paper 30 or more of the art terms, phrases, vocabulary words, and artist names that were covered and ask students to respond to five questions using as many items from the list as they can. The five questions require personal response and connections to the work covered in that unit. One of my first exams includes the question "How has art broken (and how does it break) boundaries across cultures, societies, and generations?"

Other assessments include observation, sketchbook-workbook review, checklists, and oral communication. The summation pieces are graded by criteria and a rubric scale with a weight of 30%, whereas the rest of the portfolio has a 70% value. Each mini-unit is assigned 100 points, the fourth unit 200 points, and the ensuing individual student projects 300 points. This encourages students to produce more than one student-initiated project before the end of the semester.

Since changing my approach from the traditional teacher-guided, lecture-style instruction method to this Creative Process format, I have had more positive engagement from all students in all class periods. My discipline problems are almost nonexistent. Student initiative outside class has increased. I have only a few students who still need to be encouraged past trite and clichéd content. And, best of all, I have few students who choose to slide by with minimum effort.

Helpful Tips

In the first few days of the semester, there is a frenzy of drop-add activity. I do not issue brushes and paints until students are ready for the summation or final piece. It is very efficient to have students snip color swatches from old magazines and use glue sticks with heavy drawing paper as the first support. The composition and brush technique practices can be done on drawing paper and glued into their sketchbook-workbooks.

Students are required to supply their own sketchbooks by the end of the second week of class. I supply the painting supports for the mini-unit summation paintings. The first three mini-unit paintings are done on illustration board or mat board scraps, size 5 by 7 inches or 6 by 8 inches. Students are required to supply their painting supports for the major projects that follow the mini-units. The first brush application technique I introduce is flat, well mixed. Beginning with this style gives students the experience of careful mixing and both the rate of drying and the change in hue as the paint dries. They need this experiential information as the brush application techniques increase in difficulty. For mixing the paint, I distribute tongue depressors that were discarded in bulk by a local medical facility when their shelf life expired. I issue styrofoam dinner plates that I buy inexpensively in bulk at a local discount store. Students keep their styrofoam palettes in extra-large ziplock storage bags, which I also purchase in discount bulk packages.

🕊 Choose Adventure

Nancy J. Pudas
Eden Prairie, Minnesota

What makes a good physical education program these days? I believe that the answer is *choice.* The physical education program at Eden Prairie High School is designed around that concept. When students register for 9th grade, they are given a choice of registering for 1 of 15 physical education electives. In 10th grade, they choose 1 of 16 electives. Each student must complete one class in 9th grade and one class in 10th grade. Classes are 86 minutes long and are taken for a 9- to 10-week quarter.

These elective choices range from dance to weight training, from individual sports to team sports at the competitive or recreational level. Because students are given so many choices, we have very few problems with attendance, attitude, or participation. At the core of our program are our state standards, which require a student to show competency and knowledge in two physical activities, in one aerobic activity, and in their own ability to create a fitness plan based on the FITT principles spelled out in the standards.

We also offer a strong elective program in 11th and 12th grades. Here, students choose from 17 electives, again ranging in content from weight training to team sports to outdoor education. We are most proud of this outdoor program, and it is therefore the one that I talk about here. It is the one that has brought us statewide recognition.

We have chosen to incorporate adventure into our outdoor program, and to this end we have designed courses that focus on team building and risk taking. We use icebreakers to get students to know each other and feel comfortable with each other. We use trust activities to encourage students to put their physical and emotional trust in others. We use communication activities to enhance their ability to communicate thoughts, feelings, and behaviors more appropriately.

We focus on group decision making in a series of graduated activities. We set group goals that lead to action and to an understanding of what one can and cannot control. We use many of the activities that were developed by Project Adventure and described in their *Silver Bullets* book (Rohnke, 1984). A second series of books that we use is the two volumes of *Team Building Through Physical Challenges* by Glover and Midura (1992). Over a week is spent on our low-ropes course, challenging students to do their best to solve group challenges on elements such as a Spider Web.

Our fall outdoor course includes two weeks of these introductory activities. Then we begin a unit on backpacking. Many hands-on activities are incorporated. Students learn about all necessary equipment and how to pack it in a pack. They practice making meals on various stoves, learn to purify water, and set tents. They make survival kits and practice imaginary survival situations. They also learn to use a map and compass. The class culminates with a three-day trip (over a weekend) to a state or national park.

Upon returning from this trip, the students learn rock climbing. We built an indoor rock wall about six years ago, and it is truly loved by our students. We have six climbing stations. Students are taught the necessary knots and belay techniques as well as climbing skills.

In the spring, our outdoor education classes include units on canoeing and kayaking, snorkeling, fishing, and camping. A weekend trip is also taken in this class. This time it is a whitewater rafting trip.

Creativity and innovation in program design are so important. We believe that we need to provide opportunities for students to branch out and find an activity that they will embrace for the rest of their lives so they will be healthy adults.

Helpful Tips

1. *Brainstorm*—Ask the kids what they would like to do if money were no object (I bring a speaker in on parachute jumping and one on kite flying).

2. *Dream*—What would you like to teach?

3. *Think*—What is your environment conducive to (we ski here, too)?

4. *Ask* for money and fun programs.

5. *Compare* your budget to that of other departments, and compare the number of kids you serve. What do they spend on textbooks? Do you have a curriculum cycle such that extra funds come your way every so many years?

6. *Fight* for what should be yours.

7. *Write grants*—Somewhere out there is money.

8. *Collect donations*—Some families are done camping and have leftover equipment, or they don't use the treadmill or exercise bike they bought with good intentions.

9. *Get a bus driver license*—It reduces the cost of your field trips and creates flexibility.

References

Rohnke, K. (1984). *Silver bullets*. Dubuque, IA: Kendall/Hunt.

Glover, D. R., & Midura, D. W. (1992). *Team building through physical challenges*. Champaign, IL: Human Kinetics.

CHAPTER **9**

Topic Smorgasbord

Sharing More Key High School Issues and Perspectives

T his chapter offers a variety of helpful information from your colleagues.

⬚ Chapter Overview

■ **Karla Mullen,** an English/social studies teacher at Watertown High School in Watertown, Wisconsin, asks, "Which is more memorable, a lecture on architecture or a visit to a neighborhood where the architecture is found?"

■ **Debbie Kelley,** a family and consumer science teacher/teen parent coordinator at the New Direction Learning Center in Keller, Texas, explains how she lives her mission to make a difference in the lives of our teenage parents and their children.

■ **James Wade D'Acosta,** a social studies teacher at Fairfield High School in Fairfield, Connecticut, feels that teachers can tackle controversial topics and films more easily during field trips than in whole-class settings.

▨ Making Community Connections

Karla Mullen
Watertown, Wisconsin

Many people remember a cherished time in school that usually came at the end of the school year: the annual field trip. This experience was often so rich in social and academic learning that it stands out among all the school days as special and memorable. Contemporary neuroscience helps us understand why these days remain in our memories long after the teacher's name or the textbook's lessons are lost to us. When people learn in an environment that creates context, the lessons stay. For example, which is more memorable, a lecture on architecture or a visit to a neighborhood where the architecture is found?

Science tells us that our brains are at their most efficient and receptive when all the senses are stimulated. Complex and challenging situations, consequently, result in the highest levels of learning. In other words, we now know that learning is a highly social activity that requires construction of knowledge, not simply transfer of knowledge from teacher to student. With this in mind, I have developed a strong "go to it" basis for my curriculum. I teach interdisciplinary English and social studies classes: American Studies, combining American literature and history, and World Studies, combining contemporary world literature and history. Because my classes are two periods in length, I have the benefit of taking students out of the school during my class periods, without their having to miss other classes. Here, I share some of the community-related activities that I use.

Most of the connections we make in these courses are to our local community. We live in a small midwestern city of about 20,000 people. There is a large retirement village in our town, and that is the source of some of our best ongoing connections. For example, when we study the geophysical and cultural differences in the various regions of the United States, we invite senior citizens who have traveled or lived in another region to serve as consultants on a project related to a particular region.

The students design museum-style exhibits, and the seniors serve as sources of information. They often have photographs and souvenirs from their travels, which they "loan" to the students to use in their exhibits. One woman who lived in Alaska for 20 years brings in many beautiful Inuit objects, which the students use for their displays. On the day that the displays are ready, these "consultants" are invited to the opening, which is held in the library.

Similarly, in a unit on war and peace, the students visit the retirement village to interview the residents about their memories of Pearl Harbor. When possible, we do this on December 7, the actual date of this historic event. Almost everyone there has some memory of that day, whether they fought in the war or served on the home front. The students interview the senior citizens and then write both a thank-you note and an article for a booklet that we assemble called "Memories of War." Copies of the booklet are placed in our school library and in each of the residences at the retirement village. We also have visited the senior citizens in the spring, when the students have a long list of topics they have studied (e.g., the Depression, the wars, various presidential campaigns, and the McCarthy era).

They ask the seniors to recall their memories of any of these events. One year, the local newspaper ran a series based on the articles my students wrote, which the newspaper called "Bridging the Generations." My students loved seeing their work in print, and I had many comments from appreciative citizens who enjoyed this trip down memory lane.

When I first planned this activity, many of the senior citizens were reluctant to participate; their view of teenagers had been formed by media news, which portrays teenagers as out-of-control, vulgar, drug-taking creatures. The teens, on the other hand, thought anyone over 50 had to be a relic who didn't have a clue. However, after participating in the exchange, they are always mutually, pleasantly surprised. Sometimes, an ongoing relationship forms between the groups. Consequently, whereas the benefit to learning is great (because these people have the "real-life" stories to share), there is another benefit in the building of bridges between the generations.

When we study environmental issues in a thematic unit called "America the Beautiful," my students are asked to develop a project in which they improve our town environmentally. Over the years, the students have taught lessons about environmental awareness to grade school children, worked on a prairie restoration project, explored environmental issues locally, or worked in a peace garden in our school, which is a student-managed project. Again, the connections between age groups create a positive experience. Additionally, a higher level of environmental awareness between the students and the place in which they live is fostered.

Early in the World Studies class, in order to bring home the extent to which the global economy affects all our lives, I send my students out into the community in small groups to visit local businesses and determine to what extent the global economy affects our town. They must call for an appointment, and then, with a list of questions in hand, they go to the businesses to find the answers.

They want to know if the businesses import or export any products, how international business is actually conducted (e.g., how money is exchanged, and how prices are set), and other related questions. Some of the students visit grocery stores or chain stores and ask permission to record the source of products there. The students are always astounded at the extent to which our small town is involved in the global economy. This awareness contributes to their realization that they can no longer stay ignorant of the issues of the world in which they live.

I like to build on relationships with grade school and middle school children, especially because we know that younger students often idolize the high school students. Last year, my students organized and managed a millennium essay contest for all the local grade and middle schools. They made a plan, deciding on the theme "My Dreams for the New Millennium."

Then they formed teams to visit the schools and promote the project. Later, they dealt with the daunting task of reading hundreds of responses and picking the winners at each age level. Finally, they had the joy of awarding the monetary prizes to the children. The winning essays were placed in a city-sponsored time capsule, to be opened in the year 2100.

In the spring, my American Studies class does a study of local history. As part of that study, I take the students on a "Yellow Bus Tour" of the town. Early in the unit we study the Native Americans who lived here long before the Europeans arrived. Then we learn the story of how the place was settled by Europeans, find out about some of the famous and infamous people who lived here, and learn about various immigrant groups and why they came here. We study architecture and local industry. Then, with an itinerary in hand, we ride through the town to see the sights. Often the students will disembark to walk through an older neighborhood or to have a close-up look at, for example, the work done by the Works Progress Administration in one of the local parks during the Depression. Students often say this trip gave them a fresh look at a town for which they had previously had little appreciation.

One of the best ways to build connections to the community is through inviting guest speakers to class. We use firsthand accounts from community members about World War II and Vietnam. We invite a local historian to share his collection of old pictures of the town. I invite the head of the local Chamber of Commerce to talk to the students about the city in which they live. They get to see the promotional video the city uses to attract new businesses. Foreign exchange students, immigrant students, and migrant workers are all invited to come into our class.

In World Studies, I always invite people of different religions to come in and share their stories with us during our quarter-long study of the major world religions. During this study, I also take the students to visit a Buddhist temple, a mosque, a synagogue, and a Greek Orthodox church in a nearby city. Peace Corps volunteers give an intimate portrait of developing nations that no textbook can give. Even though we live in a small town, the resources are really limitless, and what we can't find here, we look for in neighboring larger communities.

In the World Studies class, we do an I-Search (Macrorie, 1988) paper during the first quarter in which the students are asked to deal with the question "What will I do when I graduate from high school?" I take all the students on a field trip to Madison, Wisconsin. Some of the students visit a large university there, some go to a small private college, and some visit a large technical school. Many of my students have never been on a campus before and have had trouble picturing themselves being in that place. This experience opens their eyes to the possibilities before them.

I also encourage the students to do job shadowing and to use the extensive resources of the Internet in assessing skills and finding information of jobs and schools. The I-Search format lends itself to the kind of lifelike research that most of us do throughout our lives, as opposed to the more esoteric research writing that is commonly done in the classroom.

Finally, I think the best connection we make is through a video-conferencing and e-mail project with an urban school. My school is made up of almost exclusively white children. We have a small number of Hispanic students and a handful of foreign exchange students; thus, my students often lack the experience of interacting with minorities. Several years ago my school was chosen to be an Ameritech Super School, which meant that we were given a ton of technology. Part of this grant was a videoconferencing television. I found a teacher at a predominantly African American urban school who was interested in the project also. Each year, we start out getting acquainted by introducing ourselves with a 25-word autobiography or an autobiopoem. We occasionally do this via e-mail or directly during a videoconference. Then we "meet," usually biweekly, to answer questions, share projects, or have discussions about issues ranging from current events to racism.

In the fall, the students from the city visit our school for a day, during which they attend some classes, tour the school, share lunch, and usually are entertained by some kind of show or demonstration. We sometimes have a scene from the school musical, a karate demonstration (we had a world champion in our school for a while), or singing or dancing by some of the students. This year we are collaborating on an art project, which we are calling "Tag Match." With the help of the art department, all the students will "tag" a large canvas. Then the canvas will be cut into two pieces; one piece will stay in our school and one will go to theirs.

In the spring, we visit their school. They usually share music by their gospel choir or demonstrations of ethnic music and dance by their immigrant students, and we visit classes and tour their school as well. The culminating project is the publication of a combined newspaper. This is the fifth year for this activity, and the other teacher and I always come away with a feeling of gratitude for the spirit of our students and their willingness to bridge that terrible racial divide that seems to permeate our culture. Invariably, the students discover that people are the same, that the dreams and fears and joys they have as teenagers are the same, regardless of background, color, or creed.

Over the years I have done other projects like this one with South Bronx High School (an e-mail project in which we read the same books [*Malcolm X* and *Canterbury Tales*] and shared responses and made a publication together). Another project I did was with an urban grade school, where we played the roles of famous people found in their social studies textbook and then the little kids "interviewed" the characters played by my students. It was great fun to see the eyes of the children as they "talked" with Benjamin Franklin or Pocahontas (played by a squatty male football player from my class—this at the time when the Disney version of Pocahontas was popular!).

Another project I did involved an e-mail and video exchange with Aoyama University in Tokyo, Japan. Their students were interested in working on their English, so we sent e-mail to them, to which they responded. Then we exchanged videotapes based on the idea of "A Day in the Life of . . ." We showed them life in our little town: on the farm, in the school, in the shops, day care centers, nursing homes, and around the town. We learned from them about crowded transportation systems, Buddhism, and the use of American products in television ads in Japan (heavily geared toward tobacco and alcohol). There is a Web site managed by St. Olaf College that lists international projects if you are interested in pursuing this avenue.

All these experiences build on the concept of learning in context and provide frameworks from which students can expand their understanding. The students always enjoy this type of learning and seem to remember the experiences in detail. Although planning these activities is time consuming, the results are well worth the effort.

Helpful Tips

1. Students need clear guidelines for how the experience will be used in future classes and what type of assessment is to be expected. Writing assignments, from thank-you notes to business-style reports, from articles for newspapers to personal reflections and e-mail, all enhance the processing of these experiences, as well as giving an opportunity to write for real audiences, for real purposes, in appropriate forms.

2. When you plan your curriculum, think in terms of simple, local contacts that you can use. Parents are great sources of information and contacts. For the religious sites trip, I contacted a religious roundtable group that put me in contact with

a person who helped enormously with names and phone numbers.

3. Be sure to acknowledge people who help with your trips. Simple thank-you notes from students, or combined thank-you responses that I type and send, mean a great deal to speakers and tour organizers and keep the doors open for the next school year.

4. The costs of bussing can sometimes make taking trips difficult. I have gotten help with funding from our gifted and talented department and from parent organizations, and I have even sought small grants. Sometimes, the senior citizens visit us, instead of our going to their village.

5. Teach the students how to look someone in the eye and introduce themselves. We rehearse this skill, even though my students are 16 to 18 years old. Sometimes, they have not had to address a stranger and do an interview, or perhaps they have not had to write a thank-you note that has good detail. One of the best features of this type of curriculum is that one is given an opportunity to teach more than textbook content. On the visits to the mosque, temple, or synagogue, the students are reminded to be reverent in others' places of worship, even if they have been required to remove their shoes and sit on the floor or to do some other thing that feels "foreign." These skills carry over into many situations.

6. Wherever possible, involve the students in the planning: How shall we handle lunch? Should we go here first, or later? Who would like to plan the food for our guests? What music shall we play during the planting of the prairie celebration? Would it be better to go on a Friday or a Wednesday?

7. This is probably pretty obvious, but I like to send letters home to parents about our plans. In my school, we have to have

permission slips for every trip away from school. Informing parents of the plans and the connection to the curriculum gains support for the projects.

8. Standards from the state in which I live are supported in innumerable ways by these types of projects. For example, in Social Studies, a major standard is that students need to understand their own historical roots to gain perspective on the present. Another key standard focuses on Native American history in the state. By holding debates and discussions with people of diverse ethnic backgrounds, students learn to defend a position, make ethical discriminations, and learn tolerance, behaviors that are reflected in multiple standards as well. A major emphasis in standards relates to understanding concepts of production, distribution, exchange, and consumption in the world economy.

9. Within the discipline of Language Arts are standards related to the writing process, collaborative writing, and writing for real audiences and for real purposes. Interdisciplinary standards are found both locally and in many national standards, such as the National Council for the Social Studies standards and the National Board for Professional Teaching Standards. Finally, standards relating to social behaviors are emphasized in many documents, from making contributions to one's community to understanding and practicing social etiquette, such as making introductions and writing thank-you notes.

In this kind of deeply contextual teaching and learning, one touches upon so many of the standards, both for students and for teachers. But most important, these types of activities address what we know about how people learn, instead of focusing on the sterile, sequential impulses sometimes fostered by aligning standards with curriculum.

Reference

Macrorie, K. (1988). *The I-search paper.* Portsmouth, NH: Boynton/ Cook.

▧ Teenage Parents and High School: A Partnership for Success

Debbie Kelley
Keller, Texas

Almost everything in life seems to come with two parts: the good and the bad. For teachers, one issue that seems to prove this point is dealing with teenage pregnancy. The good news is that teenage pregnancy is on the decline. The bad news can best be explained by presenting a few statistics and facts.

In the United States, nearly 1 million teen girls become pregnant each year (Alan Guttmacher Institute, 1999), with about half resulting in a teen birth (National Center for Health Statistics, 2000). To put this in perspective, 1,403 girls give birth each day! The consequences of teenage parenting are great for both mother and child. A teenage mom is 30% more likely to drop out of school (Alan Guttmacher Institute, 1999), and 80% of teen mothers ultimately receive public assistance at some point (National Campaign to Prevent Teen Pregnancy, 1999). Teen mothers are also more likely to be unemployed or to earn less than other employed women who are not teenage mothers (American College of Obstetrics and Gynecologists, 1997). Yet the teen parent is not the only affected member of the parent-child relationship.

The consequences of teen birth for the infant are also dramatic. The babies are more likely to be of low birth weight than other infants, and they have a greater chance of having developmental problems (Annie E. Casey Foundation, 1998). Infants of teen parents are also twice as likely to live in poverty and are more likely to be victims of abuse (Annie E. Casey Foundation, 1998). As children, they are 50% more likely to have to repeat a grade level in school (Annie E. Casey Foundation, 1998), and female babies are more likely to become teen mothers themselves (Alan Guttmacher Institute, 1999). As these statistics show, teen pregnancy and parenting are issues that deserve attention. My purpose here is to briefly describe the components of a teen parent program and show how a partnership between teenage parents and high school correlates with student success!

As a Teen Parent Program coordinator in a typical suburban school district, it is my mission to "make a difference" in the lives of our teenage parents and their children. Education is the key to unlocking the door of hope for the future in the lives of teen parents and the next generation, their children. To achieve the goal of educating teen parents, we must create programs to serve these students.

Why should school districts develop special programs to serve pregnant and parenting students? Because we are in the business of educating our nation's children! When a school "allows" a parenting student to "fall between the cracks," it reduces the opportunity for that student to lead a productive and self-sufficient life. In turn, the infant of that same teen parent will also become a student in a few short years. We all know that a child is more successful in school when the parents have experienced success in school. By showing concern for this vulnerable student population, we can make a difference in the lives of teen parents and their children. The impact of our support must not be underestimated! Our job as educators of teen parents is complex. Not only do we have the job of teaching our students, but we must also help teen parents achieve physical and emotional well-being.

A pregnant or parenting teenager typically has feelings of isolation from classmates. More than likely, that student previously experienced low self-esteem, which is now intensified by the pregnancy. The parenting student not only manages school but now must balance the increased demands of caring for a baby, being a family member, and working a part-time job. Teen parents must balance all these demands while still trying to grow up and take care of their own personal needs. In some cases, teen parents find themselves parenting their children while also trying to reparent themselves.

It is understandable that the expectations of school attendance, homework, and a scholarly attitude quickly become secondary to meeting the needs of a physically, as well as emotionally, demanding daily life. It is imperative that pregnant or parenting students enter into a supportive partnership with school if there is to be success.

A school district has a variety of ways to set up a program for teen parents. In a small program, a teacher or counselor can meet with a student periodically at lunch, before or after school, during an activity period, or during a class period. Ideally, a daily class period could be scheduled so that student parents would meet each day for a parenting class and to provide a support network for one another.

Pregnant and parenting students may be served at a traditional high school, a school within a school, or at an alternative campus. Frequently, a smaller alternative campus is more accommodating to the individual needs of the student. In our school district, pregnant or parenting students may choose to transfer to our alternative campus, New Direction Learning Center (NDLC) or to remain at their home campus.

As teacher/coordinator of the Teen Parent Program at our alternative campus in the Keller School District, I meet with students every day during a scheduled class period. As the Keller School District Pregnancy-Related Services Coordinator, I also make regular visits to the two traditional high schools to see pregnant and parenting students who have elected to continue their education at those schools.

For a school to provide additional programs for student success, there must be appropriate funding. Once again, the size of the school district and the program's needs will determine the cost. A school district may apportion program funding through local, state, or federal school funds. In Texas, a student receiving pregnancy-related services generates weighted funding for the school district. There are state and

federal grants that may also be accessed by application. The community is another resource for financial support, as well as being a pro-
vider of nonmonetary assistance.

Corporate and foundation grants also provide a wide variety of
funding opportunities. An excellent book for funding sources and
program development is *Books, Babies and School-Age Parents* by
Lindsay and Enright (1997) from Morning Glory Press. Once a
school makes a philosophical and financial commitment to become a
partner in success with teen parents, decisions about program components must be made.

Of course, education is the groundwork of any school program.
For teen parents, there may be a choice between an academic curriculum that could lead to college and a career and technology program
that leads to employment. Education in parenting skills is also critical
and an essential component of a teen parenting program. With a teen
parent course, we can share information ranging from having a
healthy pregnancy to child development and positive parenting,
which are some of the essential goals of the program.

In terms of curriculum, states vary in the availability of a teen
parenting course. In Texas, a school district may request approval
from the Texas Education Agency to teach an innovative course titled
Parenting Education for School-Age Parents I and II. The Texas Education Agency allows the district to individualize this course to meet
student needs and grant between one half and two elective credits toward graduation. An excellent curriculum for this course, *Successful
Parenting for School-Age Parents,* has been developed by the Home
Economics Curriculum Center at Texas Tech University in Lubbock,
Texas. Another excellent source of curriculum for teen parent education is Morning Glory Press (telephone: [714] 828-1998). I use a
combination of both resources when teaching teen parenting at
NDLC.

There are many components that contribute to the success of a
teen parenting program. Counseling services need to be made available
for teen parents. Access to career, academic, and personal guidance is

fundamental for student success. Teen parents are often intimidated by the maze of social agencies that are able to provide assistance. A counselor can help students by coordinating agencies to maximize resources.

Another facet of counseling is the support group. Teen parents face feelings of isolation from peers, so a support group of other teen parents brings students with similar situations together for "sharing time." By doing so, teen parents can learn and relate with their peers, ideally reducing their feelings of isolation and cultivating their self-esteem and confidence.

Two other components that contribute to a successful teen parent program are child care assistance and transportation. These components are so necessary for teen parents and their success. Child care and transportation eliminate common roadblocks for teen parents, allowing them to have a better chance of succeeding in a teen parent program. Minimally, a program can assist a student in accessing these services, whereas another program may provide one or both at no cost to the student. Child care and transportation require a substantial financial commitment from a school district, but they are both so fundamental and critical to the positive achievement of the student.

In conclusion, I feel that the essential component of an effective teen parent program is the teacher. As teachers, we must serve not only as educators but also as advocates for our young parents. Many times, an academic teacher does not have the opportunity to interact on a very personal level with a teen parent. Frequently, many teachers are completely unaware that the student is a parent. We as teachers spend more hours each week with students than any other adult. Therefore, it is incumbent on us as teachers to be sensitive to the great demands placed on these young parents and to serve as mentors.

It is our job and purpose as educators of teen parents to establish a program that benefits all students within our reach, regardless of students' personal situations. If we can develop a successful and productive relationship between high schools and teen parents, in turn we will have created a partnership for success.

Helpful Tips

The Role of Community Service in Your Teen Parent Program

Several years ago, I accepted the role of community service sponsor at NDLC and organized opportunities for students to participate in community service. Among other projects, we walked in the March of Dimes Walkathon, did yard work for the elderly in Keller, and collected food and clothing for the Community Storehouse.

Our teen parents regularly participated in activities at our neighboring nursing home. Some of these activities included assisting with the monthly birthday party and celebrating holidays and special events with the residents. Occasionally, the teen parents would take their babies and toddlers to the nursing home. It was so touching to see the warmth and joy on the face of elderly residents when they would lovingly snuggle a small child in their arms.

As a teacher and sponsor, I see a direct relationship between community service and the classroom, especially at NDLC. An alternative high school of choice, NDLC is where students have elected to attend because they have experienced the difficulty of "fitting in" at a traditional high school. Many of the students are personally disadvantaged by such conditions as being teen parents, having health problems, being victims of abuse, being economically disadvantaged, living on their own, being academically disadvantaged by being behind on credits, or being attitudinally disadvantaged.

Obstacles that often affect this student body are limited personal resources, lack of support, and low self-esteem, which affect school performance. Many of our students see themselves as victims, and participating in a service project enables these students to look "outside" their own situations.

When students participate in community service, the benefits are great:

1. Personal growth and development through improved self-esteem; self-responsibility; moral development; reinforced values and beliefs; and exploration of new roles, identities, and interests

2. Social growth and development through improved social responsibilities and concern for others, civic participation, understanding the appreciation of people from a wide range of backgrounds

3. Intellectual development and academic learning through improved basic skills, including expressing ideas, reading and calculating, higher-level thinking skills such as problem solving and critical thinking, motivation to learn, insight, judgment, and understanding

New Direction Learning Center has been recognized for the past three years by the Meadows Foundation for our contribution to the community, and we received a $500 grant each of those three years to continue our work. When a student participates in community service, not only are there great personal rewards, but a positive, healthy, and caring school climate is fostered. Community service and interaction with others can provide a positive influence that can enable a teen parent's success.

References
Alan Guttmacher Institute. (1999). *Teen sex and pregnancy* [On-line]. Available: www.agi-usa.org

American College of Obstetrics and Gynecologists. (1997). *Strategies for adolescent pregnancy prevention.* Washington, DC: Author.

Annie E. Casey Foundation. (1998). *1998 Kids Count report* [On-line]. Available: www.aecf.org

Lindsay, J., & Enright, S. (1997). *Books, babies and school age parents.* Buena Park, CA: Morning Glory Press.

National Campaign to Prevent Teen Pregnancy. (1999). *Facts and stats* [On-line]. Available: www.teenpregnancy.org

National Center for Health Statistics, Centers for Disease Control and Prevention, U.S. Department of Health and Human Services. (2000). *Birth data and rates, 1990-1999* [On-line]. Available: www.cdc.gov./nchs

Field Trips

James Wade D'Acosta
Fairfield, Connecticut

CHALLENGES

1. Missing classes in order to go on a field trip creates more pressure and work for students, many of whom have part-time jobs and considerable extracurricular hobbies and obligations.

2. Teachers endanger their jobs when they chaperone school trips. The older kids get, the more trouble they are prone to get into. Teachers are at maximum vulnerability during overnight trips. Let's face it, we live in a litigious society.

SOLUTIONS

1. High school students, especially juniors and seniors, are young adults. Many are hard at work searching for meaning in life. They have a serious, mature side that will respond to serious, mature opportunities.

2. Thanks to interstate highways and coach buses with VCRs, teachers can run highly effective, tightly focused, one-day field trips to locations within a 300-mile radius of their school.

ADVANTAGE

Because field trips are voluntary excursions requiring parental permission, teachers can tackle controversial topics and films more easily during field trips than in whole-class settings.

EXAMPLES

Gettysburg

Gettysburg National Military Park in Gettysburg, Pennsylvania, is 270 miles from my school in Fairfield, Connecticut, or 540 miles round trip. The location is worth the effort for many reasons: location of the largest battle ever fought in North America, connections to slavery and every other imaginable Civil War topic, site of Lincoln's immortal address, and accessibility of the ground itself to students. I go a few weeks before teaching the Civil War in class.

Schedule. Leave by coach bus at 5:45 a.m. Show Ted Turner's production of *Gettysburg* on the bus using its VCR capabilities. It's a very long movie perfectly suited for the bus ride and for introducing students to the battle. Arrive at about 11:00 a.m. Students have until 1:00 p.m. to view the excellent museum and bookstore in the visitor center and to eat lunch. From 1:00 p.m. to 6:00 p.m., students walk, hike, and scramble all over the battlefield during a professionally led tour. The bus is used to shuttle the group across long distances.

Highlights include climbing among the boulders of Devil's Den, scrambling up the hill at Little Round Top, marching in formation across the field of Pickett's Charge, and listening to a recitation of Lincoln's address in the graveyard among the remains of those who "gave the last full measure of their devotion." The trip back is anticlimactic, but I take the opportunity to show Kevin Costner's *Dances With Wolves* because it ties into the Civil War and goes far more deeply into Native American culture than I do in class. We arrive back in Fairfield at about 11:00 p.m.

Washington, D.C.

Washington, D.C., is 300 miles from my school or 600 miles round trip. It has a lifetime of suitable attractions and educational opportunities, so the question becomes one of focus. I take students to Washington, D.C., in order to confront the best and worst in human nature and to instill some good old-fashioned patriotism into their souls. I go for the National Holocaust Memorial Museum and for the Vietnam Veterans Memorial Wall.

Schedule. Get on the bus at 5:30 a.m. Show *Life Is Beautiful* and *Schindler's List.* Arrive in Washington, D.C., at 11:00 a.m. Grab a bite to eat and then spend two and a half to three hours in the Holocaust Museum. Students walk through and touch the sides of a box car used to transport men, women, and children to a death camp. Inevitably, some students are descendants of Holocaust survivors. Out of the museum by 3:30 p.m. Chaperones divide with groups and then disperse among the other museums on the Mall.

At 5:30 p.m. the large group reassembles at the Vietnam Veterans Memorial Wall. Students run their fingers along the deeply etched letters of the names of those who did not return. A contemplative moment and some sincere words are in order on the steps of the nearby Lincoln Memorial. At 6:00 p.m. we board the bus for home. I show *Full Metal Jacket* and *Good Morning, Vietnam* as introductions to an upcoming unit on the 1960s. Students arrive back in Fairfield at about 1:00 a.m. happy to be alive.

Religion: A Controversial Topic

Many social studies and English department courses cannot be well taught or understood without the inclusion of religion. Religion is a motivating force or an excuse in nearly every historical event and a recurring component in the literature of every nation. Furthermore, students confront religion when their classmates die and when any number of other tragedies occur. Should they attend the wake or the funeral? What is "paying a shiva call"? Why do bad things happen to good people? Students want to know the answers to such questions, yet this topic is nearly untouchable in public schools.

Field trips carry parental approval and therefore provide an excellent opportunity to tackle this topic using local resources, especially for teachers working in or near cities. In one day, from 7:30 a.m. to 4:00 p.m., I take students to one-hour sessions in each of five different houses of worship representing the largest Western religions: Judaism, Christianity, and Islam. Students visit the sanctuaries of representative congregations and interact with professional clergy. Question- and-answer periods further personalize the experience and allow for the inclusion of current events such as hate crimes and suicides. American History classes investigate the leadership of religious institutions in historic and ongoing civil rights movements. Western Civilization and Politics classes focus on the beliefs and symbols of Jews, Christians, and Muslims. Students often experience religious traditions other than their own for the first time. They gain precious insights that help them cope with difficult and awkward situations throughout their lives, from interfaith marriages to funeral customs to understanding holidays such as Ramadan or Yom Kippur.

National Standards

Field trips in general fulfill Standards IV and VI of the National Early Adolescence/Social Studies-History Standards in my state. Standard IV is "Advancing Disciplinary Knowledge and Understanding: Accomplished teachers have a repertoire of strategies and techniques that engage student interest in and advance student understanding of United States History, World History, Economics, Political Science, and Geography." Standard VI is "Developing Civic Competence: Accomplished teachers develop in their students the knowledge, skills, and attitudes necessary to be responsible citizens of a constitutional democracy." Being there makes a huge difference. Each field trip deepens a student's understanding of the diverse lifestyles and opinions of our citizens and their individual responsibility in upholding constitutional freedoms.

It is also important to realize that many students will not take another history or social studies course after high school. Even those who do take one or two courses in college are highly unlikely to be offered field trips. If we want students to visit historic sites and museums as adults we should model that behavior while we still have the chance.

Helpful Tips

Visit congregations that are familiar to your students.

Consider timing the trip close to Passover and Easter. The rabbi you use may be willing to conduct a model Passover Seder during lunch. Do as much "touch" and "see" as possible. Ask the imam to lead students through a call to prayer, the rabbi to open a Torah scroll, the Catholic priest to display the Eucharist, the Protestant minister to explain the absence of Jesus from the cross. Publicity takes the issue of tolerance of religious traditions beyond the bounds of the school and into the wider community. This trip is an attractive news item, and local reporters may cover it from several different angles over the years.

Conclusion

I wanted to create a "high school" network. This is the result of many phone calls, e-mails, and faxes. I hope you enjoyed this award-winning material as much as I did!

Index

CORWIN PRESS

The Corwin Press logo—a raven striding across an open book—represents the happy union of courage and learning. We are a professional-level publisher of books and journals for K–12 educators, and we are committed to creating and providing resources that embody these qualities. Corwin's motto is "Success for All Learners."